SAMUEL SEABURY
PRIEST AND PHYSICIAN
BISHOP OF CONNECTICUT

(Courtesy of Yale University Art Gallery)

Duché portrait of Bishop Samuel Seabury
Copy made by Mildred Jordon

SAMUEL SEABURY
PRIEST AND PHYSICIAN
BISHOP OF CONNECTICUT

by
Herbert Thoms, M.D.

1963
THE SHOE STRING PRESS, INC.
HAMDEN, CONNECTICUT
LONDON, ENGLAND

Library of Congress Catalog Card No: 63-12263
Printed in The United States of America

Dedicated to

The Rt. Rev. Walter H. Gray, D.D.

Bishop of the Diocese of Connecticut

CONTENTS

FOREWORD

by
Edward Rochie Hardy,
Professor of Church History,
Berkeley Divinity School,
New Haven, Connecticut

Samuel Seabury, Bishop of Connecticut (and Rhode Island) is well known to members of the American Episcopal Church as the first bishop of their church, and the bearer to the United States of the apostolic succession in the Christian ministry as the churches of the Anglican Communion have received and preserved it. But his official and symbolic significance has often unfairly distracted attention from his individual achievements and his personality. He was an earnest priest and pastor, a physician of bodies as well as of souls, and, as his sermons and other writings show, a theologian of no slight learning and ability. Loyalty seems to be the keynote of his character – loyalty to the ancient church and its faith, loyalty to his vocation and ministry, loyalty to his King, as a conscientious British subject, and then after Great Britain had renounced its rights over the thirteen colonies loyalty to the new state and nation with which he gladly threw in his lot. If both as priest and bishop he sometimes displays a human tendency to stand on his rights and expect recognition of his status, this reminds us that he was no bloodless paragon but a real man. His ministry fell in difficult times, during the troubled years before the Revolution, and then after it in the period of slow recovery of the church which he loved; unlike William White he did not survive beyond the day of little things into the period of growth and expansion for which his labors helped to prepare the way. Of White and Seabury an old Connecticut churchman well said that White was persistently gentle and Seabury gently persistent. Among the first bishops of the Protestant Episcopal Church in the United States of America White and Seabury were the two great men and great Americans (of Provoost, at least in his relation to Seabury, the less said the better); each of them left a great heritage behind him to the life of the country as well as to the church.

There have been several formal studies of Seabury the churchman and the bishop. Attracted to the field by his interest in early American physicians, of whom Seabury was one (although unhappily we know few details of his activities in his second profession), Dr. Thoms has been moved to produce a more informal account of Seabury the man and the American. I am glad to welcome this happy addition to the Seabury literature.

Stony Creek, Connecticut
    All Saints' Day
    November 1, 1962

ACKNOWLEDGEMENTS

I am deeply indebted to Professor Edward R. Hardy of
the Berkeley Divinity School for reviewing the text of this
book and for furnishing much significant information from
the storehouse of his extensive knowledge. The deep interest
of Bishop Walter H. Gray of the Diocese of Connecticut also
finds reflection in these pages particularly those devoted to
existing relations between the Connecticut and the Scottish
Church. The dedication of this book to him is but a small
token of my appreciation of unstinted time afforded me in
conference and correspondence. Other members of the Episcopal Clergy have been most helpful, in particular, the Reverend Sherrill B. Smith, Sr. of Brooklyn, Connecticut and the
Reverend C. Lawson Willard of New Haven. I owe a debt of
gratitude to custodians of certain Church structures in particular those associated with the following, The Glebe House,
Woodbury, Trinity College Chapel, Hartford, St. James's
Church, New London, the Berkeley Divinity School, New
Haven. Their ever-willing courtesy to the stranger within
their gates has been to me a witness of the fine spirit within
the Church Organization.

Institutions which have given valuable service include,
Sterling Library, Yale University, Berkeley Divinity School.
The Yale Art Gallery, New Haven Colony Historical Society,

Frick Art Reference Library, University of Aberdeen.

I tender thanks to John and Frances Ottemiller. Over a period of years our relationships as author and publisher have never strained, but added to, an abiding friendship.

Herbert Thoms

INTRODUCTION

My interest in Bishop Samuel Seabury started at the
time I discovered he was one of the 18th century Doctors of
Yale College, and that he was trained in medicine at Edinburgh and practiced that art to some extent most of his life
and assiduously so at periods. In according him a chapter
in my book bearing the above title I did so because he is a
great American that many of us know too little about.

My present purpose is to recount his history in a shorter
memoir than either of the two biographies acknowledged as
authoritative, namely, that of E. E. Beardsley, published in
1881, and that of W. J. Seabury, published in 1908.

My story deals chiefly with the dramatic events in Seabury's life which eventually led to the first Episcopate in
America. I have also attempted to fit Seabury the cleric physician into the medical picture of his time. I have drawn
freely from the Seabury letters used by these authors but
there are other areas of historicity which have yielded information which I believe will augment their studies.

With most of our cleric physicians in New England medicine was something of a handmaid in the curing of men's
souls. There is a good evidence that Samuel Seabury went
beyond this and taught medical students during his sojourn
in New York at the time of the Revolution. He is a figure in

American medical history although his presence here is greatly overshadowed by his prominence as a religious leader and theologian.

Samuel Seabury, Bishop of Connecticut, is to be remembered as an important figure in our history as a nation; as one whose dedication and unswerving loyalty to his life's work was never questioned even by his enemies and one in whose faith we can find strength for our own.

Herbert Thoms

SAMUEL SEABURY
PRIEST AND PHYSICIAN
BISHOP OF CONNECTICUT

Chapter One

THE REV. SAMUEL SEABURY OF HEMPSTEAD

When as America's first bishop the subject of this
memoir followed conventional Church custom and signed
his letters simply as Samuel Bp. Connect., his enemies accused him of putting on airs and some of his friends thought
that it was a little too much side for sober New England. It
is doubtful if such things ever bothered the Bishop for dedicated as he was to His Master's cause he was equally inbued
with the responsibilities of high station in the Apostolic
Church and the dignity which centuries had accorded his office. Every inch a soldier in the battle for men's souls
Samuel Seabury stood up to full height as a bishop.

Born in an obscure village in colonial Connecticut, that
son of a Congregational minister would one day appear before the seats of the mighty in the Mother Country and occupy
the highest position of her Church in America. He would also be branded by fellow countrymen as a hated and trouble-
some tory and for safety's sake be forced to seek shelter
within the British lines. His story is one of trial, sacrifice
and struggle which finally led to triumph. It is expressive
of the finest in human dignity and of amazing courage.

As has been mentioned, Samuel Seabury was not born
into the Church but shortly after his coming into the world,

his father of the same name, resigned his pastorate with
the Congregationalists at North Groton and proceeded to
London to take Holy Orders in the Church of England. His
defection was largely due to the influence of his wife and
her relations who were staunch Episcopalians but some
seeds of questioning may have been planted within during
his student days at Yale College. It was while he was there
in 1722 that the Rector, Timothy Cutler, and the only tutor,
Samuel Browne, precipated an explosion in that academic
environment by declaring themselves for the Church of England. Shortly after this, the father of the future bishop
enrolled at Harvard and at a later date the Rev. Timothy
Cutler sponsored his application for Holy Orders in the
English Church.

Events leading up to what happened at Yale are relevant
to the story of America's first bishop for there were others
beside Cutler in the Yale family who would have influence in
the affairs which would concern Samuel Seabury, the younger.
The beginnings of the English Church in Connecticut remain
in a good deal of obscurity until the turn of the 18th century.
Indeed, until 1708, nonconformity to the Congregational
Order was subject to punishment by the law of the land. It
was in that year that the Connecticut Assembly passed what
was called an Act of Toleration by which persons in the Colony could obtain permission to worship God in their own way

by appearing before the County Court and there declare
their "sober intention." As citizens they were still obliged
to pay for the support of the Congregational Churches.

Such relaxation of Puritan vigor was no doubt prompted
by what was going on within the Colony. Almost twenty
years before, in the Town of Stratford a number of free-
holders of the faith of the Church of England had expressed
a desire to worship in the faith of their fathers. They, of
course, had no minister but did gather for private reading
and private use of the Liturgy. Of great importance for
them and others of their faith was the establishment in London in 1701 of the Society for the Propagation of the Gospel
in Foreign Parts, known familiarly as The Society. Among
its first acts was the sending to Connecticut and other British colonies in America a missionary to travel about and report back to the Society.

The man selected for this duty was George Keith who
for twenty years had been a leading light among the Philadelphia Quakers. He had separated from them in 1694 and
proceeded to England for Holy Orders. Subsequently the
Society took him up as a missionary and with an assistant,
the Rev. George Talbot, the two travelled in the colonies
keeping a record of activities and observations. The only
town in Connecticut which they visited was New London
where they passed a Sunday and preached at the invitation

of the Rev. Gurdon Saltonstall, afterwards governor. According to their report, "He civilly entertained them at his house and expressed his good affection to the Church of England." The report also stated that at the time in Connecticut there were, "Thirty Thousand souls (in) about thirty towns, all Dissenters, (Congregationalists) supplied with ministers and schools of their own persuasion."[1]

An important figure in the early day Connecticut Church was Colonel Caleb Heathcote, a layman residing in New York who was interested in establishing the Church in Westchester and western Connecticut. In 1701 he prompted a group of worshippers at Stratford to make application to the Bishop of London for a missionary to that place. Three years later the Rev. George Muirson was sent to a similar post at Rye, New York. In 1706 he and Heathcote visited the shore towns from Greenwich to Stratford. It is recorded that they rode into the latter village with the Colonel fully armed, "having been threatened with prison and hard usage." While at Stratford, Muirson preached and baptized twenty-four persons.

A few months later the two revisited Connecticut and again experienced hostility, persons being warned against attending any Episcopal assemblies under a threat of a fine of five pounds. In Stratford some members of the Congregational Society were said to have welcomed "the sound of the pure and fervent Liturgy," and the minister there, Mr. Reed, to have expressed a willingness to receive Holy Orders if it could be arranged. Heathcote in a letter to the Society told them, "There is a very ingenious gentleman at Stratford, one Mr. Reed, minister of that place who is very inclinable to come over to the Church ... being by much the most ingenious man they have."[2] For some reason Reed never went to England but lost his pastorate and was obliged to leave the territory.

The Church, however, was gaining a foothold in Stratford for at the time of the visit of Muirson in April 1701 the group had organized themselves into a parish with wardens and vestrymen and Muirson himself hoped to be transferred there. A friend in London applied to the Society in his behalf but by the time the transfer was made Muirson had died. The developments at Stratford from that point on begin to have increasing interest for us for the next move of the Congregationalists to combat and destroy the growing interest in the Church was to invite the Rev. Timothy Cutler of Boston, one of the best preachers in New England, to come to them. For the next ten years he remained with them, his learning and reputation becoming widely and favorably known, so much so, that in 1719 he was invited to become Rector of Yale College. He was then 35 years old.

A student impression of the new rector has been left to us by young Jonathan Edwards, later to be famous as a

theologian and President of Princeton College. Writing to
his father he reports, "Mr. Cutler is extraordinarily cour-
teous to us, has a very good spirit of government, keeps
school in excellent order, seems to increase in learning, is
loved and respected by all who are under him."[3] Under
President Cutler, as he was then called, the College prospered but in the Spring of 1722 rumblings of stormy times
ahead began to be heard. In May or June, the Reverend
George Pigot, an Episcopal missionary arrived at Stratford.
Shortly afterwards he wrote to the Society at London that he
had had a conference with Rector Cutler and five other Congregational ministers and all were, "determined to declare
themselves professors of the Church of England as soon as
they understand they shall be supported at home."[4] The
five referred to were outstanding ministers in the Connecticut Colony, John Hart of East Guilford, (Madison), Samuel
Whittelsey of Wallingford, Jared Eliot of Killingworth,
(Clinton), James Wetmore of North Haven and Samuel Johnson of West Haven. All were graduates of Yale College.
For some months the group, with Timothy Cutler and Samuel Browne, had been meeting in the College Library and
elsewhere to discuss matters of doctrine, especially ordination. It seems more than likely that the meetings were
instigated to a considerable extent by the Rev. Samuel Johnson who over a period of years had been taken with the

beauty of expression found in the Book of Common Prayer.
For a number of years he had possessed a copy given to him
by Samuel Smithson of Guilford who as an immigrant had
brought it from England. Smithson was the father-in-law of
the Rev. Jared Eliot. It is reported that on occasions the
phraseology of Johnson's public prayers reflected the words
of the Prayer Book. According to the Church historian,
Beardsley, the Book was placed, "into the hands of the youth-
ful Johnson before he left his native town, and he read it and
reread it until his mind was charged with its contents."[5] It
is not at all improbable that Jared Eliot might have suggested
the gift as a guide to the young minister's thoughts. Johnson
had been a pupil in Eliot's school at Guilford and no doubt
was an attractive and able pupil.

A climax to the deliberations of the group came on the
evening of Commencement Day, September 12, 1722, when
with President Cutler and Tutor Browne the group proposed
to the College trustees that on the next day they would hope
to discuss with them certain questions regarding the validity
of the Presbyterian ordination and the claims of Apostolic
succession. So it was that following dinner on the 13th a
meeting was held in the College library at which the ques-
tioners announced that, "all were seeking light on the duty of
entering the visible communication of the Church of England."
The effect of this says Ebenezer Baldwin, "created great

surprise in the minds of the people and the Trustees, as
there was not at the time a single clergyman of the Episcopal order in the Colony."[6] This was putting it mildly for
nearer the truth were the words of President Woolsey of
Yale spoken years later who said, "Greater alarm would
scarcely be awakened now, if the Theological Faculty of the
College were to declare for the Church of Rome."[7]

Before the end of the meeting the presiding officer,
Governor Saltonstall, proposed that the "friendly argument"
be posponed until a later date. On October 16, another meeting of the minds was held and at that time Johnson stood
alone with Cutler and Browne. Wetmore followed his example a few months later. Cutler was immediately "ex-
cused" from the rectorship of the College and Browne
resigned. All three went to England together and there received Holy Orders. Cutler returned to become the Rector
of Christ Church, Boston, and Johnson to open at Stratford
the first Episcopal house of worship in the Colony, 1724.
James Browne died of smallpox in England and was buried
there. Of the group of seven ministers Johnson and Eliot
rose to greatest distinction in their respective denominations
and in collegiate affairs. Johnson became the foremost
leader of the Church in the Colony and went on to undying
fame as the first president of King's College, now Columbia.
Eliot became famous as a physician as well as a Congrega-

tional minister.   He was a friend and correspondent of
Franklin and as a scientific agriculturist wrote the first
book on that subject published in the colonies.   The College
honored herself and him by making him the first of her graduates to be a member of the trustees.   For many years he
occupied the honored senior position in that group where
his tolerance in matters of religion was in striking contrast
to some others including President Elisha Williams.   To
Johnson and Eliot go the credit for obtaining the munificent
Berkeley gifts for Yale College.

The reverberations of what a Harvard historian has
called the "earthquake at Yale" spread to all parts of the
Colony.   Not only the legislature but the people became interested and the students themselves took sides in natural
sequence.   Within the next twelve years fourteen young men
who graduated at Yale came into the Episcopal Church most
of them for a time having officiated as Congregational ministers.   To be added to these, though a nongraduate, was the Rev.
Samuel Seabury, the father of the future bishop.   He had been
sent to Yale to prepare for the ministry by his father Deacon
John Seabury of North Groton.   When as a student this young
Samuel came home from the 1722 Commencement we may be
sure there was paternal concern about the goings on at that
occasion.   Doubtless Deacon John talked the matter over with
his pastor the Reverend Woodbridge for it is noted that the

next summer the minister's son Dudley and young Samuel
entered Harvard together.

It was from Harvard College that Samuel Seabury, the
elder, received his Bachelor's degree in 1724 and later his
Master's. At the age of twenty he came the first pastor of
the Congregational Society at North Groton and about the
same time married Abigail Mumford the daughter of Thomas and Hannah Mumford of New London, both members of
the Episcopal group of worshippers there.

On November 30, 1729 their second son, Samuel, the
future bishop, was born. Two weeks later he was baptized
in the First Congregational Church of Groton. It was not long
after this that the father resigned his pastorate at North Groton and went to England for Holy Orders. Accompanying his
application to the Bishop of London were letters of recommendation from the Rev. Mssrs. Timothy Cutler, Samuel
Johnson and James McSparran. The latter, Episcopal missionary at Rhode Island, was related by marriage to Thomas
Mumford. At a later date when the New London Parish was
formed under McSparran, Thomas Mumford was chosen first
warden.

Samuel Seabury of North Groton received ordination at
the hands of Bishop Edmund Gibson of London on August 21,
1730. He was then appointed Missionary at New London by
the Society with an annual salary of £ 50. He arrived there
the following March.

The use of the word missionary in the early American Church needs some clarification. Because of the wide and sparse distribution of the settlers in the colonies and the comparatively small numbers of members of the Church among them, the idea of the missionary preponderated in the minds of the English Church authorities. The chief responsibility of the Episcopate in America rested with the Bishop of London. It was to aid him and provide for its support that the Society for the Propagation of the Gospel in Foreign Parts was organized. With them the word missionary was used in a wide sense for ordinarily he was only sent to places where worshippers had grouped themselves together either having a church building or the hope of soon having one. Many men sent out by the Society were not merely missionaries but priests in charge of parishes.

On Easter morning, April 10, 1732 the small group of Episcopalians at New London met and organized the Church there electing Thomas Mumford as Warden. He continued to be either a warden or vestryman for the next twenty three years. While their rector Samuel Seabury had been abroad his wife Abigail had died and on his assumption of duties at New London he and his two sons, Caleb and Samuel went to live in a house built by him on State Street not far from his Church. It was here in order to help out his small stipend as Rector he kept a grammar school.

The next year on May 27, 1733 the Rector at New London married Elizabeth the daughter of Adam and Esther
Powell of Narragansett, the Rev. James McSparran performing the ceremony. Seabury's preaching extended beyond his
own parish doing so occasionally at Norwich, and regularly
at Hebron. Six years later in 1739, the Anglican revivalist
George Whitefield was attracting much attention in the colonies.
Rector Samuel Seabury regarded him as a trouble maker
and denounced the antics of the itinerant preachers who followed him. While Whitefield had been in New London, Seabury informed the Society the town had been in a turmoil.
Years later his son was to have similar feelings about the
same revivalist.

In 1742, Samuel Seabury of New London asked the
Society to be transferred, telling them that the people of
that town, "consisting generally of poor people", could not
support a priest and a church. When the pulpit at St.
George's in Hempstead, Long Island, became vacant he was
sent there at the request of that parish. The worshippers
there were apparently more affluent for they built a house
for him and he prospered in other ways. He owned two
slaves, was able to practise medicine to some extent and
also kept a school for "young gentlemen at his own home in
a genteel manner at £ 30 per year, schooling, washing and
wood for school-fire included."[8] There is mention in his

diary of giving thanks to God for having won L500 in a lottery. The idea of keeping slaves may be a surprise to some
but good authority states that in that time about 4500 slaves
were owned in Connecticut and 5200 in Massachusetts.

In June 1763 the Rev. Samuel Seabury of Hempstead
sailed for England where he remained for some months. On
returning he landed at New London and again preached to his
former congregation adding another segment to a circle
which was to come into fulness by his son and grandson who
both occupied the Rectorate at St. James's Parish, New London. He died at Hempstead, Long Island, June 15, 1764.

Samuel Seabury, the father, was a very important influence in the life of his son, the Bishop, because of the un-
usually close relationship between them. Their years
together as adults were more than are given to most fathers
and sons. In the latter part of the father's life the son occupied a parish in nearby Jamaica drawn there by filial devotion. During that time they saw each other frequently
and they had much to talk about for in addition to their
church duties, they were school teachers, medical practitioners and both ran farms. The Puritan stock which they
shared was of the best. The father of Deacon John Seabury
was a physician and surgeon at Duxbury, Massachusetts, and
his mother was Elizabeth Alden (Seabury) grand-daughter of
John and Priscilla (Mullens) Alden.

What came after the Samuel Seaburys, father and son, is worthy of note. As we have seen, the son of the Bishop, the Rev. Charles Seabury followed him in the pastorate at New London. Charles' son, another Samuel, held the Rectorate of the Church of the Annunciation Parish, New York, for many years. He was succeeded by his son the Rev. William Jones Seabury, the author of Memoir of Bishop Seabury. William comes down to our own time in his son Justice Samuel Seabury of the New York Supreme Court, champion of human rights and of good government.

Chapter Two

YOUNG SAMUEL SEABURY

When the Rev. Samuel Seabury moved to Hempstead,
Long Island, his son Samuel was eleven years old. It was
there in his father's school and under his tutoring he prepared for college. The school was a valuable contact for
him with boys of his own age and social status. With the
parents preoccupation with the parish, the school and the
farm, a large family of boys and girls, there is little
chance that young Samuel was much pampered even though
he was selected to follow in his father's footsteps. We
would like to know more about the family life and particularly about the mother who no doubt had much to do with the
various enterprises. We can visualize young Samuel as a
rugged, muscular type of boy excelling in games requiring
endurance and strength. All through his life he had splendid
health. In middle age he is described as, "Stout, robust and
massive", characteristics which his later portraits show.

Neither of Seabury's principal biographers have anything to say about his college career which means that it is
likely that no intimate records exist. We can, however,
from some sources learn about his college mates and the
environment in which he spent most of the years from 1744
to 1748. Some of the young men who were attending Yale

College at that time were to become valued and close frie
of Samuel Seabury the younger. Chief among them was J
miah Leaming of the Yale Class of 1745 who declared for
Church while at college and later served the Church at N
walk, Connecticut, for 21 years. Regarded as a tory at
time of the Revolution, Leaming was arrested and for a t
kept in the County Jail, an experience which resulted in a
illness which left him permanently crippled. In July, 177
his church and a great part of the houses in his parish we
laid in ashes at the British invasion of Fairfield County u
der General Tryon. Leaming himself lost everything and
was taken by the invaders to New York where he remaine
for the rest of the war. His estate was confiscated by th
Americans. Jeremiah Leaming comes in and out of the
story of Samuel Seabury as an important figure.

Of equal prominence in Seabury's later affairs was
Leaming's classmate, Thomas Chandler. Just after graduation he declared to enter the priesthood of the Church of
England, studying with the Rev. Samuel Johnson and later
becoming a catechist at St. John's in Elizabeth, New Jersey.
Three years later he was ordained by the Bishop of London
and returned to Elizabeth as Rector. In 1775, he, too, was
obliged to take refuge behind the British lines and soon
sailed for England where he remained ten years. After the
war the see at Nova Scotia was offered to Chandler but his

health was too far gone for him to accept. He returned to his old parish and nominally, at least, to the rectorship there. One of Seabury's classmates who had an unusual career in the Church was John Ogilvie, probably born in Scotland, who after receiving Holy Orders became a missionary to the Mohawk Indians. Later he became assistant minister at Trinity Church, New York and aided in publishing the Book of Common Prayer in the Mohawk language.

Others of Seabury's college mates included William Sturgeon who after receiving Holy Orders returned to be a priest at Philadelphia. He did not live to see the Revolution. Prominent as lay Churchmen were William Smith who became Chief Justice of Canada and Enos Alling of New Haven who became warden of Trinity Church there, and its largest benefactor up to his time.

Classmates prominent in national affairs were Lewis Morris, Lyman Hall and Oliver Wolcott, all signers of the Declaration, and Naphtali Daggett, Ezra Stiles, prominent in affairs at Yale and in Connecticut.

When Samuel Seabury entered Yale College in 1744 at the age of fourteen the president was the Rev. Thomas Clap who is credited with introducing science into the curriculum. He also had ideas of making the College a university but for many years it was still to maintain most of the aspects of a theological seminary. One of the early accomplishments of

the Clap administration was the adoption of a new set of laws
for the College, setting down rules for governing students
and covering every imaginable deviation from virtues esteemed important to the Puritan mind. Practically every
waking hour of the student was regulated; study periods,
lectures, and religious exercises. Even his language was
prescribed. Article 10 of Chapter III states, "Every student
in this College, shall in his ordinary Discourse Speak in the
Latin Tongue; and the President and Tutors may at their Dis-
cretion enjoyn the Observation of this Law by Some Proper
and Reasonable Penalties."[1] A portion of Chapter IV contains this catalogue of misdemeanors; viz; "Fighting, Striking, Quarrelling, Challenging, Turbulent Words or Behaviour,
Drunkenness, Uncleanness, Lacivious Words or Actions,
wearing woman's Aparrel, Defrauding, Injustice, Idleness,
Lying, Defamation, Tale bareing or any such like Immorali-
ties."[2] All were punishable by fine, admonition or expulsion.

One writer says that Samuel Seabury lived off-campus
which means that he lived in a rooming house in proximity
to the College. He may have lived in an Episcopal house-
hold and possibly with other students of his faith. He was,
of course, subject to all of the College Laws.

There are probably good reasons why the elder Seabury
chose Yale for his son instead of Harvard. One would be
the nearness of New Haven to Hempstead, journey by water

at that time being the readiest means of transportation.
Another, might be the liberal attitude toward Episcopalians
which existed at Yale in spite of the official adherence of
the College to the tenets of Congregationalism. In 1745, the
Rev. James Wetmore was able to report to the Society, "It
was a pleasure for me to observe at the Commencement in
New Haven ... no less than five of the Bachelors graduated
this year, openly professing the Church of England, and was
told some others of them had a good disposition towards it,
by whom we were treated very respectfully."[3]

In Seabury's senior year the digging of the cellar for
Connecticut Hall was started, later to be erected by the pro-
ceeds of a lottery sanctioned by the General Assembly. That
building is today the only remaining one of the period. A. P.
Stokes in commenting on student life of the time gives a list
of articles assigned to four students by way of dietary, namely, "for breakfast, one loaf of bread; for dinner one loaf of
bread, 2 1/2 pounds of beef, or other meat, seven or eight
pennyworth of sauce, one quart of beer; for supper, an apple-
pie (made of 1 3/4 pounds of dough, 1/4 pounds of hogs fat
(lard), two ounces of sugar, and 1/2 peck of apples), one
quart of beer." Stokes continues, "The cost of tuition was
only four shillings a quarter. There was no room rent but
merely a charge for "sweeping" of from seven to eight
pence a week. Such was Yale's simple material condition at

the time. Yet in spite of poverty, matters were conducted
in a manner befitting an academic institution, as shown by
this delightfully condescending reference to the Commencement exercises of Seabury's Class in an old diary recently
published in Massachusetts: 'Wen 14 Commencement, all
Things were carried on with utmost decency, they came
very little behind Cambridge itself.' "[4]

Under President Thomas Clap the College at New Haven
was not behind her elder sister at Cambridge in anything.
The Connecticut Legislature, now more generous in its support enabled the College to increase the number of tutors to
three. The finances were sound and in Seabury's time the
number of students had increased to 120 and others besides
himself had to live outside the College. The great gifts of
money and books from the great churchman George Berkeley, afterwards Bishop of Cloyne, had added much to the usefulness and prestige of the College and a foundation for the
teaching of science in America had been laid. The only crit-
icism that the early Yale historian Ebenezer Baldwin had of
the Clap administration was that "Poetry and belles letters
flourished feebly in a soil devoted to the culture of philosophy, mathematics and polemic divinity."[5]

At the time Samuel Seabury graduated from Yale College
his father informed the Society that a number of people in the
town of Huntington, not far from Hempstead, had conformed

to the Church and built a church where he frequently officiated and his son read prayers and sermons under his direction. In a letter written September 30, 1748 he speaks of
his plans for his son's advancement in the Church which had
taken definite form. He writes, "My son is now studying
Physic, and before he be of age to present himself to the
Society in person, I intend, God willing, that he shall spend
one or two years at Edinburgh in the study of Physic. I have
been led into this manner of educating him, from a hint taken
from one of the Honorable Society's Abstracts concerning
their designed economy of their College at Barbadoes. I
shall therefore esteem it a great favor if the Society will be
pleased to approve this method, and give him a place in their
books, and grant that he may be recommended in his favor
by our Rev^d. Commissary in regard to Huntington. My son
is not yet nineteen years of age, and as I believe he may be
employed at Huntington in reading prayers and sermons, and
catechizing to good purpose, before he will be of age for Holy
Orders, I presume to hope the Society will employ him at
Huntington with some small allowance."[6]

As a result of this petition young Samuel Seabury served
for four years in the capacity of a catechist for an annual salary of ten pounds. He no doubt also studied medicine at that
time possibly with a local doctor in addition to his father's
instruction. At the time the above letter was written the

the age for Orders as a deacon in the English Church was
21, and as a priest 24. A double journey to England for the
purpose was out of the question so the young graduate continued at Huntington until 1752 when he set out for London
bearing a letter from his father to the Bishop of London re-
iterating his plan to have the young man study at Edinburgh
for a year before going for ordination. By that time the
junior Seabury would be 24.

We know very little about Seabury's Edinburgh days.
He is said to have attached himself to the Episcopal communion while there but at that time the Scottish Episcopal Church
was almost nonexistent. Years before, severe penal laws
against clergymen had earned for them the title of non jurors by their refusal to swear allegiance to William and
Mary and their successors in the House of Hanover. The
laws were still in force and any meetings for religious worship on their part had to be held in secret. Norton tells the
story that on the first Sunday after arrival in the Northern
Capitol Seabury asked his host where he might find an Episcopal service. That worthy told him to take his hat and follow on but barely keeping in sight. After leading through
narrow lanes and unfrequented streets the young student
followed his guide to the top of a tall building where in an
upper room he found himself among a small group of worshippers. He would one day be reminded of this and similar

occasions when, in an upper room at Aberdeen Scotland, he
would receive consecreation as America's first bishop.

During his stay in Scotland Seabury undoubtedly made
friends among the Episcopal group some of whom may have
been of service to him later on. The hostile attitude which
he found in Edinburgh against members of his faith he would
also be reminded of at a later date when like them, he would
be called upon to run heavy risks due to the intolerance of
his fellow citizens.

Late in the year 1753 Samuel Seabury left Scotland for
England and on arrival in London presented his credentials
to Bishop Thomas Sherlock then occupying that see. Because of that prelate's age and infirmities, John Thomas,
Bishop of Lincoln, acted in his stead and admitted the young
American to Deacon's Orders on December 21, 1753. Two
days later Richard Obaldiston, Bishop of Carlisle, admitted
him to the Priesthood. On this same day he received from
the Bishop of London, licence and authority to become a
priest at New Brunswick, New Jersey. The Society, accordingly, granted him the appointment at a salary of £ 50
a year. That cure recently having become vacant, Seabury
was recommended for it by the Rev. Josiah Wetmore, then
of Rye, New York, whom we have met before.

Seabury arrived at his mission on May 25, 1754 and
found there a new stone church all but completed and a

congregation waiting to receive him. One of his relations,
writing about this time to another, wrote, "Mr. Samuel Seabury has returned to America again; an excellent physician,
a learned divine, an accomplished gentleman and a pious
Christian."[7]

Seabury had not been in New Brunswick many months before an occasion arose which shows something of the esteem
which his fellow priests were beginning to have for him, i. e.
his selection to preach a sermon at a convocation of the clergy
to consider the case of the Rev. John Beach, missionary at
Newtown, Connecticut who had defected from Congregationalism ten years after graduating from Yale in 1721. It was
claimed by some of the clergy that Beach's teaching with regard to the Resurrection was not in conformity with Church
Doctrine and the convocation was in the nature of inquiry into the matter. When as commissary of the Bishop of London,
Wetmore notified Seabury of his selection, he at first refused on the ground that he was the youngest clergyman in
the Provinces and some older man should be called. Years
later, at the conclusion of one of his Episcopal functions an
elderly man came up to him saying, "I have not seen you,
Bishop, since you preached at the trial of old Dr. Beach;
and I remember that, as I saw you go up into, the pulpit, I
said to myself, 'These ministers must be very careless
about their business, when they send a boy to preach for

them at such a time; but in a few minutes I found out that if
you had a boy's face, you had a man's head.' "[8]

Because of the clergy's action the Rev. John Beach appears to have reconsidered his position. He subsequently
became, "next to Dr. Johnson the ablest defender of the
Church in the Colony," and all through the Revolution he continued to use the prayer for the king standing alone in this of
all the Episcopal priests in Connecticut. President Stiles of
Yale referred to Beach as a "high churchman and a high
tory."[9]

Another and more important event in Seabury's New
Brunswick years was his meeting with Mary Hicks of Staten
Island who became his wife on October 12, 1756. She was
the daughter of Edward Hicks a retired merchant from
Philadelphia and now a widower living with his daughter and
son William. W.J. Seabury says that the young priest may
have met Mary Hicks through relations living on Long Island.
It was about the same time that Seabury was making frequent
trips there apparently with an eye on the parish at Jamaica
for he purchased a small farm there.

From the beginning, Edward Hicks was opposed to the
marriage, so much so, that he refused to sanction it. On
that account the marriage was performed at the home of the
maternal uncle of the bride, Col. William Ricketts of New
York. The groom's father came in from Hempstead to

officiate. W.J. Seabury lists four conjectures as to Mr.
Hicks' attitude, viz. 1. Personal feeling against the young
man. 2. The marriage was imprudent. 3. Hicks himself
would be inconvenienced because of financial matters.
4. Upon mere caprice.

From what occured after the marriage it is likely that
the third reason was the real one. Mr. Hicks was under
financial obligations to his daughter which he was unwilling
or unable to meet. A later claim on her part ended in the
hands of lawyers and the matter was not settled for some
years. According to Seabury, as stated by him and admitted
by Hicks the facts were that two legacies from grandfather
and grandmother Ricketts leaving to the six Hicks children
some £ 1700 had been received by Hicks and a sixth of this
sum belonging to Mary had never been paid to her.

As has been noted, about the time of his marriage Seabury was negotiating the purchase of a farm on Long Island.
In order to carry the deal forward his father-in-law had
promised him £ 400 agreeing to sign a bond for that amount
if it was borrowed elsewhere including the interest accruing.
The bond was so signed but after three years had gone by
and no interest was paid, Seabury had to pay it himself. In
the end Seabury and his wife seem to have won out, but how
much was paid is not known. One extraordinary aspect of
Hicks' defence of his actions was his clain of £ 250 for

Mary's board and clothing from the time of her mother's
death to her marriage with Seabury. What the latter thought
about that action is seen in a statement which shows his
thinking on some general principles of human behavior. An
extract reads: "Mr. Hicks has charged me £ 250 for my
wife's board and clothing from her mother's death 'till her
marriage, and in justification of this charge, says it is supported by the laws of his country. The laws of his country
I know oblige him and every man to maintain and support
his own children. It can therefore be only in some particular
cases, that the laws will permit a man to charge his children
for board and clothing, viz; when a man in unable to provide
it for them, and they have ability to provide it for themselves. But Mr. Hicks cannot say this was his case. During
the whole period for which this charge is made (which Mr.
Hicks has overrated by 14 months), he supported the character of an opulent merchant, and lived in a fashionable and
genteel manner. Those laws of his country which oblige him
to take care of his children and maintain them ought here to
take place. To these laws of his country may be added the
law of Nature, which is prior to all laws of civil Society;
and binds all parents by the stronger ties of reason and
instinct, to provide for the support of their offspring. Those
laws also of justice and humanity require that we should support those whom we have given being. The laws of the

Christian Religion lay man under the same obligations; one
of its greatest Preachers having declared that parents ought
to provide for their children and not children for their
parents. ..."10

Chapter Three

THE JAMAICA YEARS

With the consent of the Venerable Society the missionary at New Brunswick transferred to Jamaica, Long Island
in 1757 to become Rector of Grace Church Parish. He was
then 28 years old, in robust health and with a new wife to
share his labors in the vineyard. He had a home of his own
on a good farm and within easy reach of his church. He
lived within a short distance of his father and other relations,
and he and his lady were received with enthusiasm by the congregation. In addition to such blessings he was away from
the proximity of Staten Island. In spite of all that, there
were aspects of the Jamaica years that were something less
than a pleasant dream.

In the first place the difficulties with his father-in-law
in the purchase of the farm now made ownership more of a
liability than an asset. His stipend from the Society was
£ 50 and about 60 more came from the parish. The physical
aspects of the farm are seen to a considerable extent in an
advertisement for its sale in 1762 which describes, "A small
plantation half a mile east of Jamaica Village, on which Mr.
Seabury, Rector of the Church now lives. It contains twenty-
eight acres of good land, a good dwelling house (one end new),
a genteel building, a dry cellar under the whole house, a well

of good water, new barn, hovel and smoke house. There is
a fine orchard that makes fifty barrels of cider and a cider
mill of a new invention which grinds fifty bushels of apples
in one hour. Also fourteen acres of woodland two miles
from the farm, and eight acres of salt meadow that cuts
twenty loads of salt hay. Apply to the above Samuel Seabury,
Jr. who will give a good title."[1]

As a missionary of the Society twice a year it became
incumbent upon the rector at Jamaica to give an account of
his work and of parish interests. Nine letters exist which
date from October 10, 1759 to April 17, 1766. They report
baptisms, number of communicants and other details about
the town and neighboring places under his jurisdiction.
Some of them show discouragement on his part because of
lack of interest in the Church. In the first of these he says,
"Flushing in the last generation the grand seat of Quakerism
is in this the seat of infidelity; a transition how natural."[2]
In another, he tells that the people of Hempstead have shown
great backwardness in supporting their minister having
"learned from the Quakers to consider it as a mark of avari-
cious and venal spirit to receive anything of his people by
way of support."[3] In the letter of October 6, 1764 he speaks
of Whitefield's visit to the Colony which he fears has done a
great deal of mischief, "This town in particular," he writes,
"has had a continual, I had almost said a daily success of

strolling Preachers and Exhorters, the Poor Church of England is on every occasion misrepresented as Popish and as teaching her members to expect salvation on account of their works and deservings."[4] The last of the series, dated April 17, 1766 is of special interest in view of subsequent events and reads in part, "Indeed I believe one great reason why so few from this Continent offer themselves for Holy Orders, is because it is evident from experience that not more than 4 out of 5 who have gone from the Northern Colonies have returned; this is an unanswerable argument for the absolute necessity of Bishops in the Colonies. The Poor Church of England in America is the only instance that ever happened of an Episcopal Church without a Bishop and in which no Orders could be obtained without crossing an ocean of 3000 miles in extent, without Bishops the Church cannot flourish in America unless the Church be well supported and prevail, this whole continent will be overrun with Infidelity and Deism, Methodism and New Light with every species and every degree of Scepticism and enthusiasm, and without a Bishop upon the spot I fear it will be impossible to keep the Church pure and undefiled."[5]

Another source of disquiet during the latter part of his pastorate at Jamaica was Mr. John Aspinwall, a parishioner living at Flushing. The relation between the two was friendly enough at the start for Seabury has given testimony of

Aspinwall's liberality and usefulness in the Church.   In a
letter to the Society of March 26, 1761 he writes about the
near completion of the church and says, "The principal expense of the work is defrayed by Mr. Aspinwall and Mr.
Thomas Grennall, two gentlemen who have lately retired
thither.   Mr. Aspinwall has beside made them a present of
a very fine bell of about five hundred weight and I hope the
influence and example of these gentlemen in their regular
and constant attendance upon divine service will have some
good effect upon the people of that town.   Thro' Mr. Aspinwall's means also that the Church hath been constantly supplied the last half year with a Lay Reader one Mr. Treadwell
a young gentleman educated at Yale College in Connecticut of
an amiable character and disposition who intends to offer himself to the Society and with their permission go to England
next autumn."[6]

The young man, Augur Treadwell, was then 27 years
old and had graduated the year previous.   He came from a
good family in Stratford and no doubt was a very personable
young man for at a later date both Flushing and Newtown
joined in a petition to have him appointed as a missionary
and sent to them.   Seabury having jurisdictions over these
parishes opposed the appointment on the ground that the area
could not support two missionaries.   Part of Seabury's salary came from these parishes.

Treadwell received Orders probably in April 1762 and was appointed to a vacant mission at Trenton, New Jersey. Sometime in January 1763 the Rev. Augur Treadwell made a visit to Flushing probably staying at the Aspinwalls. How this visit lit the fires of controversy is seen in a letter written shortly afterward by Seabury to the Society under date of March 23, 1763. It reads, "About eight weeks ago Mr. Treadwell the Society's Missy at Trenton, New Jersey, came to this parish and passed thro' Jamaica (within three quarters of a mile of my house) to Flushing on a Saturday, without letting me know that he was in the Parish, nor did I know until two days after that he was even in the Colony. The next day the Church at Flushing was (as 'tis said) violently opened and occupied by Mr. Treadwell, the key being in my possession.

"Mr. Treadwell I am told continued there some time, preached the next Sunday after, went to New York, preached on a week day, came to Jamaica and baptized a child within a little more than a mile from my house, the child being well and several weeks old, and I had not been out of the Town for more than a day for six months; all this was transacted without giving me the least notice; either by visiting me, or by message, or by letter; nor have I either seen him or heard from him. I am utterly unable to guess at the motive of Mr. Treadwell's conduct, unless he acted under the influence and direction of Mr. John Aspinwall of Flushing ...

who has really done very considerably towards finishing the
Church and gave it a good bell, but who is disgusted with me
for declining to give Newtown and Flushing to Mr. Treadwell,
tho' I readily consented and am willing to receive Mr. T. or
any other person that shall be agreeable to the Society into
the Parish in an amiable manner; but the expenses of a
growing family will not permit me to relinquish any part of
the Salary. Nor do I conceive that I have any right to give
up any part of the Parish to the entire management of another
person, unless it should be divided by the same public authority which first established it. Had Mr. Treadwell made me
acquainted with his being in the Parish, I should readily and
gladly have invited him to preach to all three Churches, and
am very sorry he did not give me the opportunity, as it would
have prevented all disputes and a great deal of talk and noise
and ill blood. I am told that I can have my remedy at common law and have been much urged by my warmer friends to
make use of it, but I would on no account have an affair of
this kind litigated but choose to submit it entirely to the
Venerable Society, knowing that while I discharge my duty
to them, they will protect me in the quiet and peaceful enjoyment of my Mission, which I am sorry to acquaint them
is a good deal disturbed and unsettled by this behaviour of
Mr. Treadwells."[7]

If the rector at Jamaica had been willing to let the storm

blow itself out at this point it would have been better strategy
than what he actually did, which was to insert a card in a
New York paper stating that Aspinwall had at various times
traduced and aspersed his character, especially in New York.
In this broadside he informed that parishioner that if he had
any defense of his actions he might save his honor by doing
so in the public press. Aspinwall took up the challenge assuming a safe position by stating that he had been merely reported to have made verbal statements and asking point-blank
what the aspersions were. He also pointed out that the law
was open to the Rector where he could prove his allegations.

This, Seabury considered as evading the issue, which it
obviously was. Seabury, now at the boiling point, among other
things accused Aspinwall of laying schemes to drive him out
of his parish, saying, "when called upon publicly to avow
openly, and justify his assertions, (he) answers, the law is
open. The law is open, Sir!. 'Tis true, but at present it
suits ill with my purse, not with my inclination: Rest therefore in full security from a legal prosecution, and rest as
much at peace as your conscience will let you. But Sir!
Remember your evasive advertisement, can give no satis-
faction, either to myself or the Public. If you will support
the character of a gentleman, I hope you will think yourself
obliged either to deny the charge, and say you have not represented me to my disadvantage; or that you be particular in

your charge against me, and support your allegations with
proper proof; and not evade the matter either by general or
unsupported allegations, or by putting it off to some future
time."[8]

Aspinwall seems to have had the last word but it was a
battle that no one could win unless fought in the open and
that he was not willing to do. Whether one considers Seabury's language unbecoming a clergyman or not he did defend his position with conviction keeping close to the point
and demanding that his adversary do the same. As will be
seen shortly he was but warming up for the next chapter in
his life when he would be defending his Church and King.
Later too, as Bishop, there would be those who would charge
him with "having extreme views of the dignity of his office."
Whatever such views might be we can be sure that there was
never any question with him about his duty to his Church or
to Samuel Seabury, Priest. The Aspinwall controversy
reflected no credit on either party. Back of it seems to be
the fact that Aspinwall wanted to get rid of Seabury and Seabury knew it. But, the Rector was not a man to be pushed
around even a little, then, or ever.

Jamaica with its numerous administrative problems and
separated congregations, nevertheless, was giving Seabury
good experience in parish work. In 1762 he was able to report that the church was gaining strength. In Flushing the

white congregation had increased from twenty to eighty. At
Jamaica, his principal charge, one hundred and twenty
families were connected with the church. But in 1764 new
disquietude appeared on the scene in the presence of the Rev.
George Whitefield's sixth visit to America and his coming
to Seabury's parish. Here he produced the usual excitment
attending his preaching and wrote to a friend, "My late excursions upon Long Island I trust have been blessed. It
would surprise you to see above one hundred carraiges at
every sermon in the New World."[10]

As a visiting priest of the Church Whitefield was under
but little restraint. He was in no way connected with the
Society. His previous visits had been so erratic that some
of the clergy in his own church refused to admit him to their
pulpits. However earnest and zealous he appeared, he had
no warrant to neglect his ordination obligations which he did
by his disregard of the ritual and the use of the Book of
Common Prayer. In addition, he was often severe in his
condemnation of some of the missionaries in this country
making charges against them to the Society. There was no
question about his great popularity and people of all denominations came to his meetings many of which were held out
of doors. At first, his brand of Evangelism was greatly
favored by the Presbyterians and the Congregationalists but
subsequently many of them became divided in their opinion.

In Connecticut the General Association, in June 1745, had passed a resolution that, "If the said Mr. Whitefield should make his progress through this government, it would be no means be advisable for any of our ministry to admit him to our pulpits, or for any of our people to attend his adminis- trations."[11]

We have seen before what Seabury thought of him and other "strolling preachers and exhorters." Like his father he abhored any canonical and rubrical irregularities. It would be comforting for him to report to the Society, as he did after Whitefield's visit, that none of his own people were finally led astray.

Chapter Four

RECTOR OF ST. PETER'S—A WESTCHESTER FARMER

On the 15th of June, 1764, the Rev. Samuel Seabury of
Hempstead died after serving in that place for twenty years.
During the last seven the proximity of his son Samuel at
Jamaica had been of greatest comfort for the two often met
to discuss their individual and mutual problems. His successor the Rev. Leonard Cutting at the time of his appointment was serving Seabury's former rectorate at New Brunswick and was a friend of long standing. He was a graduate
of Eton and Cambridge and had taught at King's College in
New York. Cutting served the Hempstead parish until 1784.

Seabury's own position at Jamaica about the time of his
father's death had become more precarious with his growing
family and the farm not doing very well. Added to his discontent was the fact that the parsonage which had been
promised him was not forthcoming and the prospects were
poor. It was with favor and something of relief that he now
looked upon an offer from the vestry at St. Peter's, Westchester, asking him to come to them as their Rector. In
due course on December 6, 1766 the Rev. Samuel Seabury
was "admitted, instituted, and inducted," into that office by
the Rev. Dr. Myles Cooper, President of King's College and
under authority of Sir Henry Moore, Captain-General and

Governor-in-Chief of the Province of New York.

At Westchester the average congregation was 200 and in living there Seabury could be in closer touch with clerical friends in New York and New Jersey. A year after his induction Seabury wrote a letter to the Society about his situation saying, "The congregation at Westchester is very unsteady in their attendance; sometimes there are more than the church, which is a small, old, wooden building, can contain, at other times very few, generally near two hundred ... . At Eastchester, which is four miles distant, the congregation is generally larger than at Westchester. The old church in which they meet as yet is very small and cold. They have erected, and just completed the roof of a large, well-built stone church, in which they have expended, they say, seven hundred pounds currency; but their ability seems to be exhausted, and I fear I shall never see it finished ... . With regard to the income of this parish, the salary, by an act of assembly, is £ 50 currency — the exchange from New York to London being generally from £ 70 to £ 80 for £ 100 sterling. Burial fees there are here none; but the more wealthy families sometimes give the minister a linen scarf on these occasions. Marriage fees are from one to four Spanish dollars; but far the greater number go to an Independent teacher in the parish of Rye, because his ceremony is short and they have nothing to say."[1]

Seabury also reported that the parsonage house needed an outlay of £ 100 to make it comfortable and that the glebe had cost him near £ 20 to repair the fences. It seems a little strange that the Church was not better supported, for Trevelyan, in his classic history of the American Revolution, says of Westchester County at that time, "Nowhere in Europe, nor in America was there more universal ease and plenty, or a larger infusion of that natural and sincere conservatism which is based on content. Westchester County, and no wonder, was to a marked degree a Loyalist district."[2] That author gives a remarkable word-picture of the environment in which Seabury found himself; "Westchester County presented an aspect of long settled and well-ordered prosperity. The manor-houses, the bettermost of the farm houses, had nothing in and about them which was new, or cheap, or shabby. The carved wainscots; the old grates encased in tiles representing Scripture scenes, with fender and andirons of solid brass as brilliant as hands could make them; the heavy furniture of mahogany and stamped leather; the tall eight-day clocks of gilded ebony; the mirrors loaded with florid mouldings, which no one with a pure taste in art would have devised, but which, when they had hung on the wall for a century, no one who had the sense of association would ever part with; the perfection of needlework in the curtains, the screens, the cushions, and more especially the bed-quilts; the glass

cupboards with their display of antique plate, and high-
coloured Lowestoft porcelain; the Delftware, the pewter, the
copper vessels, the great wooden bowls for kitchen use, which
the Indians fashioned from knots of the maple tree; — everything was solid, everything was genuine, and, above all,
everything was scrupulously and religiously clean. For the
mansions of the country gentlemen, and the dwellings of
their leading tenants, were maintained up to a standard of
neatness surpassing the extreme point even of Anglo-Saxon
respectability. There was a very large Dutch element in the
population; and Dutch Christian names, and surnames, may
still be read in large numbers at the foot of Addresses and
Resolutions which went across the Atlantic to assure King
George of the affection with which he was regarded by his
good people of Westchester."[3]

Seabury had been at Westchester less than a year when
he was importuned to begin a mission at Johnstown, New
York, the residence of Sir William Johnson. Dr. Myles Cooper writing to Johnson in 1767 says of Seabury, "A Man of
great good Sense, of a Cheerful Disposition, and has a mod-
erate Family. ... the most suitable Person We know to live
at Johnstown. ... being a good Divine and an agreeable
Preacher, his skill in Medicines also much esteemed; his
knowledge of which Science was regularly obtained at Edinburgh."[4] However, Seabury decided to stay where he was.

At Westchester we can picture Seabury as Rector fulfil-
ling the duties of his parish, preaching and administering to
the nearby towns of Eastchester and New Rochelle, preaching
at funerals in the more remote districts, tending his glebe
and fathering his increasing family. In 1768 he had five
children, three girls and two boys. By the instructions of
the Society, missionaries were expected to set up schools
for children and in some places the Society appointed school-
masters and appropriated annually a small stipend for their
support. Such a school was in operation at Westchester under the Rector's brother, Nathaniel, who taught there until
1768 when his resignation necessitated the employing of
another man. About that time Samuel Seabury started a private school probably on the order of his father's at Hempstead. According to Vance, " 'he had more than 20 young
Gentlemen, when the Rebellion began.' Five of them were
from the Island of Jamaica and one from Montreal."[5]

Successful as many parishes were under the system and
with capable leadership, the American clergy felt that the
want of bishops not only prevented completeness of church
organization but greatly endangered the perpetuity of spir-
itual life, the Church of Christ being a Divine institution
derived from the Apostles through the Bishops who have
succeeded to their office. As early as 1750 certain propo-
sals signed by the Rev. Timothy Cutler and others were

forwarded to the Bishop of London by the Rev. Samuel Johnson of Connecticut. This paper was prepared in order to
give answer to certain misapprehensions about the settling
of Bishops in America. In England the objections to such a
course in the main were that bishops have too much coercive
power over the people in matters ecclesiastical, that supporting them was too much of a burden, and also that they
might interfere with the authority or interest of the governor or other authority of state especially where it was in the
hands of dissenters, as it was in New England.

To these objections the proposers stated that the only
power delegated to bishops was to regulate the behavior of
the clergy who were in Episcopal Orders and that, "nothing
is desired for such Bishops that may in the least interfere
with the dignity, or authority, or interest of the Governor,
or any other officer of State. Probate of Wills, licence for
Marriage, &c., to be left in the hands where they are, and
no share of the temporal government is desired for the
Bishops."[6]

In the last year of Seabury's pastorate at Jamaica the
Episcopal Clergy of the Province of New York organized
themselves for mutual counsel for promoting the Church
and particularly for furthering the movement for colonial
Bishops. It was called a convention, i. e., a voluntary union
rather than a convocation which usually connotes a superior

authority by which the clergy is called together. It was
called therefore the Convention of the Church in the Province of New York. It did receive into it members of the
clergy of both Connecticut and New Jersey men like Johnson of Stratford and Chandler of Elizabeth. Samuel Seabury
was one of the leaders and was chosen secretary. In a letter
of the Convention to the Secretary of the Society dated May
22, 1766 in reference to the loss of one fifth of the missionaries sent over by the Society, the communication says, —
"This we consider as an incontestable argument for the
necessity of American Bishops; and we do in the most earnest manner beg and entreat the venerable Society, to whose
piety and care under God, the Church of England owes her
very being in most parts of America, that they would use
their utmost influence to affect a point so essential to the
interest of the Church in this wide extended Country."[7]

This and other moves of the Convention became quite
the concern of ministers of other denominations in the colonies and it is not surprising that the Rev. Ezra Stiles, once
Seabury's tutor at Yale but now a highly influential and vocative Congregational minister at Newport, Rhode Island,
should write to the Secretary of the Convention. His letter,
dated March 8, 1768 reads, —

Reverend Sir;

The letters addressed by your Episcopal Convention to
the King's Majesty, Several Dignitaries in the Church, the
two English Universities, and to the Society, relate to a matter of public consequence, and of too great importance not
to be attended to by all America – by far the greater part of
which is, and doubtless through all American ages will continue to be Dissenters – even should the whole expanded territory from the Mississippi to the Atlantic be covered with
Episcopacy and Episcopal reverence most assuredly projected
for it. .... . The whole Dispute is now before the public . ...
if any of the transactions of your Convention should be of a
more restricted nature, yet those relative to the Prelacy and
the Imploring of Bishops cannot be such and least of all the
letters in question. According to the copies we have seen,
the Dissenters, that most respectable body in America, are
represented more by implication, as Revilers of the State,
of perverse dispositions, as dangerous to Monarchy and unworthy the King's Clemency and Protection, Our Loyalty to
the Sovereigns of the House of Hanover, our Love and Reverence for the British Constitution have been so conspicuous
that we cannot submit to be thus represented to the Parent
State. You, Sir, have said in the public prints that no such
representation has been made. It will be a pleasure, Sir,
to find your declaration confirmed by an inspection of au-
thentical copies of those seven letters. It is, Sir, for this
end that I ask them and I am sure your candor and politeness
will most freely, most readily grant my request. Though we
differ in Sentiments as to the external Policy of the Church
of Christ, yet I sincerely wish the Divine Blessing upon all
your labors in persuading sinners to be reconciled to God
and to become sincere disciples of the blessed JESUS. ...

> your most obedient
>
> Very humble ser
>
> Ezra Stiles"[8]

It was an age of letter writing, of pamphleteering, of
sharp correspondence in which opponents on political and
other questions might address each other through the private
or public press and carry on for months in verbal warfare.
Stiles letter, polite enough in its demands is, nevertheless,
a somewhat irksome letter. What he is actually saying to
Seabury is prove your words. At that time, and later, as
President of Yale College, the Rev. Ezra Stiles was one of
the great voices of freedom for the colonies. His successor
at Yale, Timothy Dwight, called him the most learned man in
America of his day and age. He does not seem to have over-
awed the Rector at Westchester, however, as Seabury's reply plainly shows. The reply which was delayed for three
months speaks not only for itself but tells a good deal of the
writer,

"To Dr. Stiles

In answer to your letter of the 8th March which I did not
receive till the 8th May I must inform you that I am precluded by a rule of the Convention from giving out any copies
of the minutes or papers committed to my care without an
order of the Convention. I have however shewed your letter
to two or three of my Brethren, and their Sentiments as well
as my own are, that the manifest unaccountable want of candor in the opposers of an American Episcopate, upon the proposed plan, is so very great, that they cannot think it a proper time to make public any of those Letters which you
mention. Several persons who were consulted with regard
to the propriety of Dr. Chandler's publishing his appeal, at
the time it was published predicted the very treatment, it,

and its author, and the whole body of the Clergy met with.
I was, I confess of a different opinion: I had such favorable
sentiments of the Candor and friendly disposition of the Dissenters, that I imagined, they would have calmly and soberly
pointed out the disadvantages they apprehended from the
proposed plan that they might have been removed. The consequence has been the plan is approved but the thing opposed.
Now to suppose an American Episcopate upon any other plan
than the one proposed, is fighting with a shadow, a mere
nonentity. But to do this in such an illiberal, abusive,
scurrilous manner as has been done here, argues so bad a
disposition, that I have no inclination to give a name to it.
The whole body of the Clergy of the Church, have been
represented by the American Whig, as Tories, that is in the
estimation of that Faction, Traitors and Rebels to their King
and country. The Convention has been represented as a
number of false deceitful men, pretending to ask for one
thing while they are really aiming at another. When I denied publicly, that any accusation was made against the
loyalty of Dissenters; I was represented as a furious fellow,
too much in a passion to know what he said— and that I really had affirmed a matter of fact, of which it was impossible
I could be a competent judge. Consider these things, Sir,
and judge for yourself, whether there is that probability of
Candour and moderation among the Dissenters, which is
sufficient to induce us to a compliance with your demand.
Far be it from me to imagine that Dr. Stiles is thus void of
candour and moderation—but then it cannot be thought that
Dr. Stiles wants those copies solely for his own inspection,
and that no other person is to see them. With regard to the
authenticity of those copies which you intimate are abroad,
I can say nothing. Those persons who know from whom and
by what means they were obtained are the best judges of that.
      And with regard to an 'Ecclesiastical Reverence most as-
suredly projected for an Episcopate, which is to cover the
whole expanded Territory from the Mississippi to the Atlantic,', I really Sir, never heard, either of such an Episcopate,
or of such a reverence.

I must also express my doubts, relating to the proceedings of all ecclesiastical Bodies being so open to public view and examination, as freely to permit copies and extracts of their proceedings to be taken. If that is the case, I would propose an expedient, that possibly would satisfy all parties, viz. let the convention and the Synod publish all their proceedings, letters, &c. and then the public would be competent judges, whether the Church or Dissenters entertained sentiments the most favorable to the universal liberty of conscience.

I have Sir, indulged the same liberty of thought and expression, which you have in your letter, and which I conclude will not be disagreeable to you. I shall conclude by assuring you that the Episcopate for America which we have so much at heart, is the plan in the appeal and no other. If there are any inconveniences which they apprehend from this plan, when they are coolly and candidly pointed out, we will join our endeavours to yours to get them removed.

> I am Sir your most obedient,
>
> humble servant

June 4th, 1768."[9]   SAMUEL SEABURY

In his position as secretary of the Convention and due to his skill in expressing himself Samuel Seabury was becoming one of the most important spokesmen for the Church. A more prolonged passage of words in which he became engaged is called the "B.W. Controversy", by W.J. Seabury, who fills up 21 pages of his memoir and then apologizes for taking up so much of the readers time. In keeping with the purpose of this book nothing further than reference will be made to that historian's full account.

The Convention of 1766 appointed a committee of two,

Samuel Seabury and Thomas Chandler, to write a publication
entitled, "An Appeal to the Public in Behalf of the Church of
England." It was subsequently written by Chandler although
Seabury is said to have seen the first draft. The Rev. Samuel Johnson called the Appeal the "best thing ever done in
America" in behalf of securing bishops. Soon after its appearance in the latter part of 1767 replies began to appear
in some of the papers, the most important appearing in
James Parker's New York Gazette under the caption of The
American Whig. They were written by Governor William
Livingston and his colleagues. They accused the Anglican
clergy of deceiving the public in the matter of the bishops
saying they wished to set up a "court favored" powerful prelate. In reply to this charge, Chandler, Cooper, Inglis and
Seabury began a series entitled, A Whip for the American
Whig, published in Hugh Gaine's Gazette, the first appearing
on April 4, 1768.

As previously mentioned quite apart from this, Seabury,
during 1768-69 was carrying on a private war with the Rev. Dr.
Charles Chauncey of Boston who had written a pamphlet in
reply to the Appeal. Seabury accused Chauncey of writing
an anonymous letter signed "B W" which were the initials of
Governor Benning Wentworth of New Hampshire. Vance says,
"The records available do not indicate the final outcome of
this controversy."[10]

Liberty, then as now, was a word of many meanings but most Americans of that day thought that their rights as British subjects were being denied by being subject to taxation without their consent. The vehement advocates for liberty, however, found little sympathy in Seabury for to him extreme measures always produced, "unbounded licentiousness in manners and insecurity to private property." He was later to suffer severely from both.

In March 1770, Seabury wrote to the Society, "The violent party heats which prevail in this Colony as well as in the others engross at present the attention of the people. ... I hope the time is not far off when these matters will be settled upon a firm and permanent foundation; but however that may be, I am confident the behaviour of the Church people, considered as a body, has been such as has done her honor, and will be remembered many years in this country with approbation."[11]

The whole substance of colonial discontent then and later on has been tersely stated by Trevelyan, "The inhabitants of New England and of Old England were made out of much the same materials; and the colonists being what they were, if certain known steps were taken, certain inevitable results were bound to follow. The question to be determined at successive points in the American controversy was in every case a clear and simple issue."[12]

The Rector of the English Parish in the Loyalist strong-
hold of Westchester, Samuel Seabury, as a man of ardent feeling was bound to be drawn into the political arena. He not
only had strong convictions in controversial matters but a remarkable capacity for forcibly expressing them. Trevelyan
calls Seabury the ablest of the tory controversialists and says,
"His character and conduct won for him in many quarters a
tribute of sympathy and respect, which gradually developed
into a sentiment little short of reverence."[13]

History shows that at the beginning, New York was
quieter and more loyal than the other colonies. Her legislature took no notice of the first Continental Congress and refused to send delegates to the second. As might be expected
Seabury was not only for the Crown but used his influence to
quiet his people and keep them from joining the Sons of Liberty. His name appears third on a list of 312 signatures
arising out of a meeting held in April 1775 making emphatic
protest and declaring, "our honest abhorrence of all unlawful
Congresses and committees, and that we are determined, at
the hazard of our lives and properties to support the King and
Constitution; and that we acknowledge no representatives but
the General Assembly, to whose wisdom and integrity we submit the guardianship of our rights, liberties and privileges."[14]

Previously, two political pamphlets had appeared in New
York without the name of the author or publisher, signed

A. W. Farmer. One was entitled, "Free Thoughts on the
Proceedings of the Continental Congress." For a time they
were attributed to Isaac Wilkins an influential and vocative
member of the loyal Provincial Assembly of New York and
an intimate friend of Seabury's. They aroused great opposition, copies were gathered and burnt, nailed to the whipping
post, tarred and feathered, indicating the treatment that the
author might expect if he should be found.

Shortly after these publications appeared came an answer
to the Farmer which was in turn answered by a pamphlet ad-
dressêd to the merchants of New York called, "An examination into the Conduct of the Delegates at their Grand Convention." This, too, was signed by A. W. Farmer who announced
that he would be pleased to defend his former publications.
The Battle of the Pamphlets was now on.

"A. W. Farmer", in other words, A Westchester Farmer, was Rector Samuel Seabury who had earlier entered
into a compact with his fellow clergymen Chandler of New
Jersey and Inglis of Trinity Church, New York, to confute
all publications which threatened the Church of England or
the British Government in America. As stated by the author,
the "Farmer" letters aimed to point out in language under-
standable by farmers and landowners, the baneful influence
which the measures of Congress might have upon them and
also that if the New York Assembly acceded to the Congress

as others had done, "They would betray the rights and liberties of their Constitution, set up a new sovereign power in
the province, and plunge it into all the horrors of rebellion
and civil war."[15]

The extraordinary power of pamphleteering which developed during the revolutionary period reflected what had
been going on in the mother country for a hundred years.
The great Johnson himself was among other things a writer
of political pamphlets. Much of the work of Defoe and Swift
took that form. According to Barrett Wendell the American
temper of revolutionary times was even more explosive than
seen in England at the time. Of many examples the destruc-
tion of the house of Martin Howard of Newport was typical.
All that tory gentleman did was to answer the pamphlets of
James Otis. Of Seabury, Wendell comments, "Though he
was an admirably devoted parish priest, nothing could protect him, an advocate of unpopular principles, from the explosive violence of the Connecticut mob."[16] The intolerance
to anything that was British became so rampant that, "Even
among Americans of high intelligence, the mere word bishop' revived in pristine fervour not only all the hatred, but
all the dread which had been excited in the minds of ances-
tral Puritans by the persecution of Laud. ... At least in ecclesiastical matters, the instinctive temper of Revolutionary
Americans remained surprisingly like that of their imigrant
ancestors born under Queen Elizabeth, "[17]

For a comprehensive study of the <u>Letters of A West-chester Farmer</u> the reader is referred to a publication of this title by the Westchester County Historical Society in 1930. In the foreword Dixon Ryan Fox says of the author The Rev. Samuel Seabury, "His clear, blunt Anglo-Saxon prose, cleaned of all encumbrance, moves forward with fearless logic. Never once, does the author forget the character he assumes, that of an intelligent, independent yeoman; the choice of words, the homely practical illustrations, the bluff frankness of the argument, are all perfectly appropriate. Indeed, as a tiller of his glebes in Eastchester and Westchester the honest rector had a right to call himself a farmer. A big and energetic man in body, a hard hitting controversialist throughout his life, his sinewy phrases are like limbs and fingers carrying the force of his personality; if ever the style is the man, it is so here."[18]

Most of the literature on both sides was published by James Rivington, publisher of the New York Gazetteer. Because of a letter appearing in that paper criticizing Isaac Sears the leader of the Liberty Boys, Rivington was branded by them as a traitor to American liberties and on November 23, 1775 his printing house on Hanover Square was completely destroyed.

One of the ablest of Seabury's antagonists in the pamphlet war was Alexander Hamilton then a student in King's College and not yet eighteen. He wrote at least two replies to

Seabury. One was entitled The Farmer Refuted: or a More
Comprehensive and Impartial View of the Disputes Between
Great Britain and the Colonies. It ran to nearly 35,000 words.
His argument was so powerful that Dr. Myles Cooper was in-
credulous that a lad of seventeen could have written them and
they were attributed to John Jay. There is a tradition that a
liberal offer was made to Hamilton to have him write in behalf of the ministry. The fact that the British Government
tried to purchase the loyalty of John Jay and others with
judgeships, in the opinion of Vance, makes the truthfulness
of the tradition entirely possible. [18]

At Lexington on the 19th of April, 1775, the War of Independence actually began and all through the colonies preparations were being made to resist the British forces. Loyalists
and patriots were becoming more clearly distinguished and
reprisals were beginning to take place. Seabury's known in-
timacy with the loyalists and his literary skill made him the
chief suspect as the Farmer, so much so that a body of colonial troops was sent to arrest him and Wilkins. The two escaped capture by hiding in a secret chimney in the Wilkins'
mansion on Castle Hill Neck where they were joined by
Chandler and Cooper, also fugitives. The house was
searched unsuccessfully but the group remained in hiding for
several days, food being conveyed to them through a trap
door in the floor. The next month Wilkins left his family

and embarked for England. A month later Seabury wrote to
him, "I hope you are safe in London; may every blessing attend you. Mrs. Wilkins was well last evening, Isabella had
a rash but is better. Everything here is quiet. ... Mr. L.
Morris has Published his remarks upon the Protest etc. —
poor me—you are safe—I think I am too. ... I think the
present scene will not last long. Drs. Cooper and Chandler
sailed last week. ..."[19]

While these two were in England they did much for Seabury. After he was forced to live behind the British lines
they secured for him a chaplaincy of a man-of-war and a
gift from a fund they had raised for needy clergymen in
America. It was due to their efforts that Oxford University
gave Seabury the degree of D.D. in 1777. In this same year
their influence is seen in his appointment as chaplain to the
Provincial Hospital in New York and his becoming a missionary to Staten Island with a salary of L50 a year. With such
aids to income and his fees from medical practice Seabury
was able to live far better than most of his brother clergymen similarly situated in the New York area.

In the beginning of the war it was inevitable that families
would become divided in their loyalties, separations occur,
and relationships become embarrassing or even dangerous.
Thus, Mrs. Wilkins, the wife of Isaac Wilkins, was a sister
of Lewis Morris, signer of the Declaration, and of Gouveneur

Morris, equally a distinguished patriot.

Seabury was not far off in his assumption to Wilkins
that the present scene would not last. Immediately ahead
trouble was waiting for him and in abundance. On the same
day he wrote the Wilkins letter he sent one to the Society,
telling them that he was "hoping to be able to keep my station. The charge against the Clergy is a very extraordinary
one, —that they have in conjunction with the Society and the
British Ministry, laid a plan to enslaving America. I do not
believe that those people who raised this calumny believe
one syllable of it, but they intend it as an engine to turn the
popular fury upon the Church, which should the violent
schemes of some of our Eastern neighbors succeed, will
probably fall a sacrifice to the persecuting spirit of independ-
ency."[20]

Writing in the guise of a farmer, Seabury's language
was designed to attract the attention of that group. Obviously
it was not that style usual with the clergy. A good example
is seen in his first paper which refers to the committee appointed to inspect the conduct of the colonists. In this he
wrote, "Will you be instrumental in bringing the most abject
slavery on yourselves? Will you choose such committees?
Will you submit to them, should they be chosen by the weak,
foolish, Turbulent part of the country people? Do as you
please; but by Him that I will not! No, if I must be enslaved,

let it be to a king at least, and not by a parcel of upstart, law-
less committee-men. If I must be devoured, let it be by the
jaws of a lion and not gnawed to death by rats and vermin."[21]

To the great credit of Seabury he stayed at his post as
long as he could with safety, serving his two congregations,
teaching his school and practising medicine to aid in supporting his family. It was while he was so engaged that, in
the fall of 1775 in November, an armed force from Connecticut came into Westchester, seized him in his school room
and carried him off to New Haven. What happened to him
on that occasion is well told in a memorial prepared by him
at New Haven and addressed to the Assembly and Governor
of Connecticut asking for his release. It is from that somewhat lengthy text that we learn what happened.

On Wednesday, November 22, 1775 about forty armed
men under Captain Lothrop appeared at the school, took him
to the parsonage, allowed him to send for his horse and then
proceeded to Eastchester where they met another company
of men, in all about one hundred. They had in their custody
Judge Jonathan Fowler of Eastchester and Nathaniel Under-
hill of Westchester. Under a guard of about twenty men the
three proceeded to New Haven arriving there three days later.
Here Seabury was kept under guard first at the house of
Captain Sears, then at Mrs. Lyman's. In both places he
was not allowed to write to anyone except to his family.

Neither could he visit his fellow prisoners. After nearly a
month of confinement, he was allowed to write a memorial
or plea presenting his case to the Assembly and Governor
of Connecticut. In this he tells about his arrest, that his
daughter had a bayonet thrust through her cap and a handkerchief which was around her neck. A quilt on a frame upon
which she was working was slashed, and his wife was forced
to open his desk from which three or four dollars were stolen.
His story continues as he says that after eight or ten days at
Mrs. Lyman's he was committed to an inn kept by Mr. Beers.
Here he was questioned by Captain Sears, Captain Lothrop,
Mr. Brown and others. They had released Fowler and Under-
hill but said they intended to keep him until the dispute between Great Britain and the Colonies was settled. When
asked for specific charges he was told there were four,
namely: 1, He (Seabury) had conspired with others to capture
Captain Sears as he was passing through Westchester and
place him aboard a British man-of-war. 2. That he had
signed a protest at White Plains against the proceedings of
the Congress. 3. That he had neglected to open his church
on the day of the Continental Fast. 4. That he had written
pamphlets and newspapers against the liberties of America.

To the first and last of these accusations he pleaded not
guilty, saying he could prove his innocence if liberated and
sent to his own province, New York. He protested that it

was a high infringement of liberty for which the Americans
are now struggling to be carried forcefully from one colony
to another for the sake of trial or imprisonment. Accordingly, "Must he be judged by the laws of Connecticut, to which
as an inhabitant of New York he owed no obedience, or by the
laws of that colony in which he had been near twenty years a
resident? ... Neither the laws of any colony nor the regula-
tions of the Congress give any countenance to the mode of
treatment he has met with."[22]

As for the accusations, the memorialist (Seabury) protested he was simply one of three hundred who had signed the
Protest and that was nine months ago. If the crime was so
obnoxious why should it remain so long unpunished and what
about the other 300? As for opening his church on the day of
the Continental Fast, he had had no notice or order other than
the common report. Also, Captain Sears had already lodged
a complaint on that score against him in New York where it
had been dismissed. Why sould he now be dragged seventy
miles from home and again impeached upon the same crime?

Seabury then describes his domestic situation, the possible ruination of his school, which in the past year had netted
him a humdred pounds, and the contracts he now had with the
parents of his pupils. Your memorialist, he continues, has
a wife and six children, to whom he owes, both from duty and
affection, protection, support and instruction. That his

family in great measure depend, under the providence of God, upon his daily care for their daily bread. That there are several families at Westchester who depend upon his advice as a physician, to which profession he was bred. That as a clergyman he has the care of the towns of East Chester and Westchester so that in his absence there is none to officiate to the people in any religious service, to visit the sick or bury the dead.

Seabury closes his cogent and scholarly argument in these words,—"He has a higher opinion of the candor, justice and equity of the Honorable House of Assembly, and shall they incline to inquire more minutely into the affair, he would be glad to appear at the bar of their house, and answer for himself; or to be permitted to have counsel to answer for him; or, in such a way as they in their wisdom shall think best, to grant him relief. And as your memorialist, as in duty bound, shall ever pray.   Samuel Seabury
Dated in New Haven on the 29th day of December, 1775."[23]

The assembly did release Seabury but not until a letter demanding that action had been written to the Governor of Connecticut by the President of the Provincial Congress of New York. He arrived home at Westchester on January 2, 1776. Eleven days later he wrote to the Society saying he was determined to stay at his mission as long as permitted to do so regardless of any personal inconvenience. Later

on he wrote, "God's providence will, I hope, protect his
Church and Clergy in this country, the disorder and confusion of which are beyond description. But it is his property
to bring order out of confusion, good out of evil; and may his
will be done."[24]

Following the Declaration of Independence on July 4,
1776, the Provincial Assembly of New York withdrew from
the support of the Crown and joined with the General Congress. The Provincial Congress now issued an edict pro-
hibiting persons to contribute in any way to the support and
comfort of the King under penalty of death. To Seabury this
edict meant the prohibition of the full use of the Liturgy which
his conscience would not allow him to use otherwise. He
directed his sexton to notify his people that he would not officiate until he was at liberty to pray for the King.

In a letter at the end of the year, dated December 26,
1776, Seabury says that after the King's troops had evacuated
Boston and the Continental Army passed from thence to New
York, bodies of from twenty to thirty men would stop at his
house insulting him, reviling the King, the Church, the Bishops, and threatening to plunge a bayonet into the breast of the
"Farmer" should he be discovered. This went on for about a
month during which time Seabury was obliged to keep out of
sight by staying away from home and returning at intervals
but for an hour or two.

Before leaving the Westchester period in Seabury's life
it may be useful to comment further on his statement that he
was "ready to vindicate his innocence" about writing the
pamphlets. We should recall that the charge was that he had
written against "the liberties of America" and this of course
he would not admit. In his own words, "If I would have dis-
avowed these publications I should have been set at liberty in
a few days; but as I refused to declare whether I were, or
were not, the Author, they kept me."[25]

When Seabury arrived home from New Haven, as he
predicted, his school was broken up and the pupils dispersed.
In September 1776 the situation become so intolerable that he
had to go behind the British lines on Long Island. In November following, his family moved to New York City. After the
Battle of Long Island and the defeat of the American forces
his position at Westchester had become wholly untenable.
Shortly after the Seaburys moved to New York, a company of
American cavalry were quartered at his residence and con-
sumed all the produce on his farm. They also burned the
pews in his church and converted it into a hospital. The escape of the family to New York was none too soon, for shortly afterward many of Seabury's parishioners were seized,
carried away and the whole region pillaged, if not by one
army, by the other.

Chapter Five

BEHIND THE BRITISH LINES

Although the American Revolution was a military struggle between the Colonies and Great Britain, it was not an
antagonism of interests or purposes but between two principles of government. In 1775-76 it was Toryism in the British government that caused the war. No political severance
would have occurred if the ideas of Walpole and Chatham had
prevailed in the Parliament. The historian John Fiske says,
"But while under the circumstances, a war was inevitable it
is only from ignorance of history that one would find in such
a war any justification for a lack of cordiality between the
people of the United Kingdom and the people of the United
States."[1]

The strong loyalist feeling in the New York area before
and during the Revolution was due chiefly to the fact that there
was the headquarters of the army and the seat of the principal
royal government in America. The Church of England was in
predominance there and it did not harbor in any measure the
intolerance towards the Puritans of New England that the
latter showed toward Episcopalism.

As an ardent loyalist it was natural that Seabury should
aid the British Army in putting down what he considered as
rebellion. When their troops passed from the Battle of Long

Island into Westchester County he presented the command
with maps and plans of the region he was so familiar with.
He knew the sentiments of his people and believed he was
right in encouraging their loyalty. It was during that period
he wrote, "Few of my people are engaged in the rebellion.
The New England rebels used frequently to observe, as an
argument against me, that the nearer they came to West
Chester the fewer friends they found to American liberty. —
that is, to rebellion; and in justice to the rebels of East
Chester and West Chester, I must say, that none of them
ever offered me any insult or attempted to do me any injury
that I know of."[2]

What went on in Westchester County after the evacuation
of the British troops embraced most of the terrors of war as
witnessed in incidents reported by Seabury to the Society. In
reporting the death of the Rev. Mr. Avery, a neighboring missionary at Rye, in a letter of March 29, 1777 he writes, "...
That evening the rebels returned to Rye, and as Mr. Avery
and many of the loyalists had shown particular marks of joy
when the King's troops came there, they became very obnoxious to the rebels, who showed their resentment by plundering
their houses, driving off their cattle, taking away their grain,
and imprisoning some of them. Among the rest Mr. Avery
was a sufferer and lost his cattle, horses, etc. On Tuesday
morning he desired the maidservant to give the children their

breakfast, and went out. Sometime afterward he was found,
some say, under a fence or in an out-house with his throat
cut, either dead or just expiring. Many people are very confident that he was murdered by the rebels; others suppose
that his late reported losses and disappointments, the insults
and threats of the rebels, and the absence of his best friends,
drove him into a state of desperation, too severe for his
strength of mind."[3]

In the same letter Seabury reports the death of another
fellow clergyman, a graduate of Yale College shortly after
himself, who was stationed at Philipsburg (now Yonkers),
and like himself a loyalist. He was seized about the same
time as Avery and carried off to the Provincial Congress at
Fishkill where he was kept a prisoner. After three and a
half months he became ill of a fever and was discharged
home with a warning to get inside the British lines. He arrived in his home in a delirium and died within a few days.

From within the city Seabury wrote to the Society, "Many
families of my parishioners are now in this town, who used
to live decently, suffering for common necessities. I daily
meet them, and it is melancholy to observe the dejection
strongly marked in their faces, which seem to implore that
assistance which I am unable to give. To pity and pray for
them is all that I can do. I shall say nothing more of my own
situation at present, than that I have hitherto supported myself

and family with decency and will not distrust the goodness of
God which has hitherto preserved me, nor render myself unworthy of it by repining and discontent."[3]

From the record we find that in November 1777 he visited
Westchester again with a view of spending the winter there but
found conditions would not warrant any such move. He then
asked the Society to be transferred to Staten Island if conditions warranted. This was granted with a continuance of his
£ 50 salary. In December he officiated there baptizing some
persons and preaching to an audience of 300. But Staten
Island was as unsafe as Westchester and he was forced to
continue in New York going on with his medical practice.

As may be imagined New York was well supplied with
clergy and Seabury, seeking for other opportunities to serve
the Church, applied for a chaplaincy in the British Army. On
February 14, 1778 he was appointed to such a post by Sir Henry Clinton in the King's Regiment of Foot commanded by Col.
Edmund Fanning. Fanning, a graduate of Yale College a few
years after Seabury as an ardent loyalist had raised and taken
command of a corps of like-minded Americans who called
themselves the Associated Refugees. After the War the
Colonel was a recipient of an honorary LL. D. degree from
Yale for his part in saving the College from ruination at the
time of the British invasion of New Haven in July, 1779.
Fanning who accompanied Governor Tryon on the expedition
was his trusted secretary.

Behind the British lines Seabury doubtless found others who had affiliations with Yale. Two months previous to his appointment as an army chaplain through the influence of his friends Cooper and Chandler, now in England, he had been given the degree of Doctor of Divinity by Oxford University.

Seabury's belief in the ultimate success of the British forces was unwavering but he wrote to the secretary of the Society in November, 1778, that the Congress was resolute and would hold out as long as they could and "it would not be supported against the vigourous efforts of Great Britain for one campaign, as the resources of this country must be nearly exhausted."[5] Shut up in New York with his family, as he was to be for the next four years, Seabury could know but little of what was going on outside either with the war or of the condition of the Church and Clergy in the other colonies. He had little to report to the Society except that his chaplaincy and medical practice gave him better opportunities to provide for a wife and six children than many of the other refugee clergymen. In one letter to the secretary of the Society he says, "Think not, good sir, that I repent my loyalty to my King, or of my attachment to the Church of England or to the British Government. Under the same circumstances I would again act as I have done even were I sure the consequences would be worse."[6]

Some idea of the false hopes that were current among
the refugees in New York is seen in letters of Dr. Charles
Inglis, Rector of Trinity Church, to the Society. On May
20, 1780 he wrote, "The rebellion declines daily and it is
in its last gasp." Two years later under date of May 6, 1782
he wrote, "Our new commander, Sir Guy Carleton is arrived
and indicates a disposition to act with vigour: and this with a
little judgment and common sense will change the fact of
things here." Apparently the group of clergymen within the
city did have some idea of what was going on in nearby Connecticut for Inglis's letter continues, "It may be some satis-
faction for you to hear that the Church of England, notwith-
standing the persecutions it suffers, gains ground in some
places, particularly in Connecticut. This I can assure you
of as an indubitable fact. The steady uniform conduct of the
Society's missionaries and of a few clergymen who are not
in their service, in that province, their adherence to the
dictates of conscience by persevering in loyalty and preaching the gospel unadulterated with politics, raised the esteem
and respect even of their enemies, whilst the pulpits of dissenters resounded with scarcely anything else than the furious politics of the times, which occasioned disgust in the
more serious and thinking. The consequence is that many
serious dissenters have actually joined the Church of England.
The increase in some places has been suprisingly great."[7]

Six months later Seabury was to report, "Both West
Chester and Staten Island remain in the same ruined state,
as much exposed to the incursions of the rebels as ever,
though these incursions have not lately been so frequent as
formerly. By what we can learn of the Society's missionaries, they seem to be in a more quiet state at present, and
suffer no personal abuse unless perhaps from some disorder-
ly individuals."[8]

It was while Seabury was pent up in New York that death
came to Mary Hicks Seabury on October 12, 1780, the twenty-
fourth anniversary of her wedding day in 1756.

During the long stay in New York Seabury's medical practice occupied a good deal of his time and was a source of
needed income. His practice in nearby Westchester to which
he has given testimony would have given him a reputation
from the start. Another source of income from medicine
would be the teaching of that art. That he did so is seen in
John N. Norton's statement in 1859; "There were living but
a few years since physicians who had studied medicine with
Dr. Seabury during his sojourn in New York."[9] Some discus-
sion of the cleric physician and medical practice deserves attention. As an entity he has long disappeared but his influence on medicine in colonial New England has not been suf-
ficiently recognised by the general historian.

ILLUSTRATIONS

All photographs are by the author unless otherwise noted. They follow in the order listed below.

Birthplace Marker

Seabury Monument, New London, Connecticut

Altar Tomb, St. James's Church, New London, Connecticut

Tablet to Samuel Seabury

Bronze Tablet, Bishop's Tomb

Glebe House, Woodbury, Connecticut

Fireplace in the Meeting Room, Glebe House

Bishop Seabury's Mitre, Trinity College Chapel, Hartford, Connecticut

Portrait of Samuel Seabury attributed to Ralph Earle

Altar used by Bishop Seabury

Chalice and Paten used by Bishop Seabury

Parsonage of Bishop Seabury, New London, Connecticut

Ordination Licence signed by Bishop Seabury (holograph)

Old Trinity Church, Brooklyn, Connecticut

Interior of Old Trinity Church, Brooklyn, Connecticut

Memorial Tablet, Aberdeen, Scotland

Bowden Hall, Roxbury School, Cheshire, Connecticut

Marker on the Site of the Birthplace of
Samuel Seabury
Church Hill Road, Ledyard, Connecticut

MONUMENT TO SAMUEL SEABURY
on
St. James's Church Grounds

(This stone was subsequently removed to the north side of
St. James's Church, New London. The inscription is largely effaced.)

On February 28, 1796 Samuel Seabury was buried in the public burying ground in New London and a table of gray marble placed over his grave with the following inscription written by the Rev. Dr. Bowden of Columbia College, New York.

Here lieth the body of
SAMUEL SEABURY, D. D.
Bishop of Connecticut and Rhode Island
Who departed from this transitory scene, February 25th, 1796
In the sixty eighth year of his age.
Ingenious without pride, learned without pedantry,
Good without severity,
He was duly qualified to discharge the duties of
the Christian & the Bishop:
In the pulpit he enforced religion:
In his conduct he exemplified it:
The poor he assisted with his charity:
The ignorant he blessed with his instruction:
The friend of man, he ever desired their good:
The enemy of vice, he ever opposed it:
Christian! Dost thou aspire to Happiness?
Seabury has shown the way that leads to it.

The
Rt. Rev. Father in God
SAMUEL SEABURY D. D.
First Bishop of Connecticut
& of the Prot. Episcopal Church in U.S.
Consecrated at Aberdeen, Scotland, Nov. 14,1784:
Died Feb. 25, 1796; aged 67.
The Diocese of Connecticut recorded here
its grateful memory of his virtues and services
A. D. 1849

On a brass plate inserted on the upper surface is an inscription in Latin of which the following is a translation:

Under the pavement of the altar, as in the final place of rest until the judgment of the great day, now repose the mortal remains of the Right Rev. Prelate, Samuel Seabury, D. D., Oxon., who first brought from Scotland, into the Anglo-American Republic of the New World the Apostolic Succession, Nov. 14, 1784. His diocese, never forgetful of the labors and trials of so dear a person, in the new Church of St. James the greater, of New London, formerly his see, now at last, after so long a time, has taken care to place this monument to his honor in the year of our salvation, 1849.

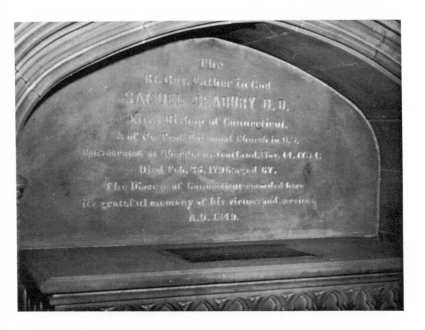

Monument in the form of an Altar tomb underneath a
canopy surmounted by a Mitre in St. James's Church,
New London, Connecticut.

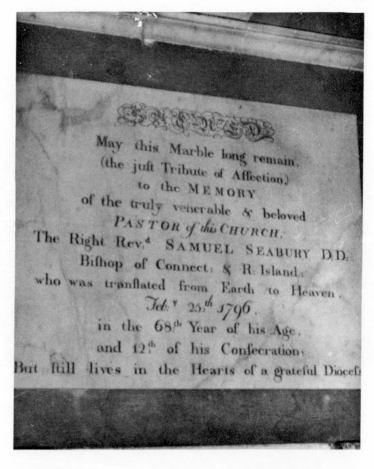

May this Marble long remain.
(the juſt Tribute of Affection,)
to the MEMORY
of the truly venerable & beloved
PASTOR of this CHURCH,
The Right Rev.ᵈ SAMUEL SEABURY D.D.
Biſhop of Connect: & R: Island.
who was tranſlated from Earth to Heaven,
Feb.ʸ 25.ᵗʰ 1796,
in the 68.ᵗʰ Year of his Age,
and 12.ᵗʰ of his Conſecration:
But ſtill lives in the Hearts of a grateful Dioceſ

Tablet marking the actual tomb of interment of
Bishop Seabury in St. James's Church, Hallam Chapel.

May this Marble long remain
(the just Tribute of Affection)
to the MEMORY
of the truly venerable & beloved
PASTOR of this CHURCH
The Right Revd SAMUEL SEABURY D. D.
Bishop of Connect. & R. Island
who was translated from Earth to Heaven
Feby 25th 1796.
in the 68th Year of his Age,
and 12th of his Consecration.
But still lives in the Hearts of a grateful Diocese.

BENEATH
THIS TABLET
LIES THE BODY OF
THE RT REV
SAMUEL SEABURY DD
FIRST BISHOP OF CONNECTICUT
AND OF THE PROTESTANT
EPISCOPAL CHURCH IN THE
UNITED STATES OF AMERICA
RECTOR OF THIS PARISH
1785-1796
HELD IN HIGH HONOR
BY ALL WHO LOVE
THE CHURCH
1926

Bronze Tablet in the floor of Hallam Chapel
St. James's Church, New London

THE GLEBE HOUSE
WOODBURY, CONNECTICUT

It was in the northeast corner room, lower floor, that was held on March 25, 1783 the historic meeting of the Connecticut Clergy.

FIREPLACE IN THE MEETING ROOM, GLEBE HOUSE

Glass case enclosing Bishop Seabury's Mitre
Trinity College Chapel, Hartford

(Courtesy Frick Art Reference Library, New York)

Portrait of Bishop Seabury attributed to Ralph Earle
now at General Theological Seminary, New York

Altar used by Bishop Seabury at New London

Rev. R. A. Hallam, one time Rector of St. James's Church, New London, gives this description in his book Annals of St. James's Church. New London. (Hartford, 1873) p. 90.

"On either side, the pulpit was enclosed by a rail that stretched across the front. Directly in front of the pulpit was the reading desk, and, before that, the holy table, which was of altar form. Some pains had evidently been taken in its construction, for its front consisted of a single board of extraordinary width. This altar is still in existence, and is in use in the chapel of the Divinity School at Middletown."

Note. The altar is now preserved at Berkeley Divinity School, New Haven, where this photograph was taken.

CHALICE AND PATEN
used by
Bishop Seabury at St. James's Church, New London
Now at Berkeley Divinity School

The inscription on the chalice reads:

Given by Doctor Yeldall
Towards making this Chalice
4 oz. 7 pwt
1773

Parsonage of Bishop Seabury, New London

Several years elapsed after Rev. Samuel Seabury, sr.
left New London before his successor the Rev. Matthew
Graves received the appointment in 1748.   In the year
previous a parsonage had been erected for the use of the
pastor on land given by Mr. Samuel Edgecomb, "4 rods
front and 9 rods deep." near the Church on Church Street.
Originally it was two stories high with a gambrel roof, a
single room in thickness, a parlor and kitchen with bed-
rooms over them and a chamber in the attic. In 1767 an
addition was made 39 feet long and 12 feet wide giving the
appearance shown in this illustration from E. E. Beardsley's biography. The house continued to be the parsonage
until 1856.

Samuel by divine permission Bishop of the — Episcopal Church in Connecticut; To our beloved in Christ William Duke, clerk, Greeting.

We do by these presents Give and Grant unto You, in whose Fidelity, morals, sound Doctrine and Diligence we do fully confide, Our Licence and Authority, to continue (during our pleasure (or till a Bishop be regularly settled in the State where you shall officiate) to whose Ecclesiastical Authority you will of course be subject) to perform the Office of a Priest in the Church of Christ, more particularly in Queen Carolines Parish in Ann Arundel County in the State of Maryland ⁎ ⁎ ⁎ ⁎ in Reading the Common Prayer, Preaching and perform...

This holograph of the licence granting William Duke of Maryland, (see p.120) to perform the office of Priest is deposited in The Yale Memorabilia Collection. The signature of Bishop Seabury appears at the left under the official seal as,– "Samuel Bp. Ep. Chch. Connect." Among his customary signatures were the following:

"Samuel, Connect.", "S. Bp. Connect."
"Samuel Bp. Connect." and "S. Bp. Connect.
& Rho. Isl."

The last listed signature appeared after he had been declared Bishop of Rhode Island in 1790.

OLD TRINITY EPISCOPAL CHURCH
BROOKLYN, CONNECTICUT

Located on Church Street, Brooklyn, Old Trinity
Church is the oldest Episcopal Church now standing in
Connecticut and the only church in Bishop Seabury's diocese which remains unchanged from his time. It was
built in 1771 by Col. Godfrey Malbone (1724-1785) and in
a considerable sense represented a protest at having his
church tax go toward the building of a church by the
Congregationalists under the lead of Israel Putnam. The
Parish has long since worshipped at another church in
the village. Old Trinity Church is today a historic
shrine kept in fine preservation through funds left for
the purpose and other aids including help from the Col.
Daniel Putnam Association. Colonel Putnam, the son
of the General, married Malbone's daughter and became
heir to his estate. He had a pew in the Church. Once
each year services are held in the Church, on All
Saints Day, November first.

One of the most notable of the Rectors of Old Trinity was the Rev. Daniel Fogg who appears elsewhere in
this book as a reporter of the famous secret meeting
of the Connecticut Clergy at Woodbury, March 25, 1783.

INTERIOR OLD TRINITY CHURCH, BROOKLYN

Nothing has been changed. The walnut panelling is
said to be the finest example of its kind in the State.

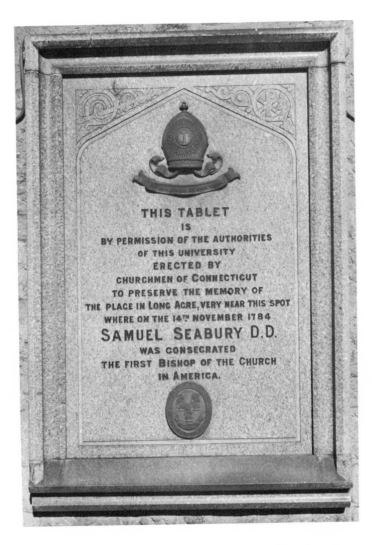

THIS TABLET
IS
BY PERMISSION OF THE AUTHORITIES
OF THIS UNIVERSITY
ERECTED BY
CHURCHMEN OF CONNECTICUT
TO PRESERVE THE MEMORY OF
THE PLACE IN LONG ACRE, VERY NEAR THIS SPOT
WHERE ON THE 14TH NOVEMBER 1784
SAMUEL SEABURY D.D.
WAS CONSECRATED
THE FIRST BISHOP OF THE CHURCH
IN AMERICA.

(Courtesy of Mr. James R. Donald of Aberdeen)

MEMORIAL TABLET TO BISHOP SEABURY
AT UNIVERSITY OF ABERDEEN
ABERDEEN, SCOTLAND

BOWDEN HALL, ROXBURY SCHOOL
CHESHIRE, CONNECTICUT

Known for a time as Seabury College this building dating from 1796 was the home of the first Episcopal Academy in New England. In 1823 the institution was changed to Washington College (Trinity) and removed to Hartford.

At a general convention of the Connecticut Diocese held in New Haven June 4, 1794 the chief business under consideration was the establishment of an Episcopal Academy to be under the Bishop of Connecticut. The first principal for the Academy chosen by the convention was the Rev. John Bowden of Stratford. Under the egis of Bishop Abraham Jarvis the Academy was incorporated as a college in 1801. Nearby is the Jarvis home built by him about 1790.

Chapter Six

SAMUEL SEABURY AND MEDICAL PRACTICE

Samuel Seabury practised medicine to some extent a
good part of his adult life. During his stay in New York he
earned much of his livelihood by doing so. He also taught
medical students there as has been recorded and he was well
equipped to do so. His having attended medical lectures in
Edinburgh must have given him a considerable standing in
medical circles. Few indeed were the physicians in all of
America at that time who had any such advantage.

Our quest in this chapter is to see how it was possible
in Seabury's day for a minister busy with a multitude of parish duties to also engage in the practice of medicine. A
good deal of conjecture is involved but by surveying something of the background of medical practice in Connecticut
we can I believe place the cleric physician into the picture
that emerges. The fact is, we know next to nothing about the
medical activities, day-to-day, of those who practised. It
seems strange that the Rev. Jared Eliot, the leading medical
light of his time, the foremost medical teacher, and a considerable writer, left to posterity hardly any evidence of the
way he practised, no medical writings, no case reports.

One approach is to seek evidence which will tell us
something of medical care in that day and those who were

responsible for such care. They were the cleric-physicians,
the regular physicians, the barber-surgeons, the midwives,
and the nurses. All had their place in the scheme of things
and all seem to have been respected.

The history of medical practice in Connecticut up to the
Revolution shows that the greatest contribution to its progress
centers around three great names, covering a period from
1646 to 1763. These were John Winthrop, Jr., Gershom
Bulkeley, and Jared Eliot. The last two were clergymen.
Winthrop the foremost scientist of his day in America, a
Trinity College, Dublin, graduate, practised extensively
in New London and New Haven and finished his days as
Governor of the Colony. Cotton Mather called him, "The
Healing Angel of Bethesda". Bulkeley, a Harvard graduate,
learned much of his medicine from his distinguished father-
in-law, Charles Chauncy, the second president of Harvard
College. He was known to be learned in medicine. Eliot a
graduate of Yale, had a father and grandfather who were
cleric physicians. The latter as the "Apostle to the Indians"
was well known for his medical skill.

As he have noted, Samuel Seabury, the elder, was
graduated from Harvard at a time when the tradition of medicine inculcated by the Mathers and Chauncy was still carried
on. He knew the importance of medical knowledge in the
ministry and no doubt sensed his own shortcomings when he

sent his son to Edinburgh, the great seat of medical learning.
But beyond the training in medicine which the young theologian might get in college he no doubt gained considerably
more from colleagues who were clerical physicians. For
example, Eneas Munson, freshly graduated from Yale five
years after Seabury, studied medicine with the Rev. John
Derbe of Southold while he, Munson, was occupying a pasto-
ate on Long Island. Later he became a distinguished member of Yale's first medical faculty.

The second of the groups mentioned, the regular physicians, were those with or without a college background who
previous to practice had served an apprenticeship with an
older physician; living in his home, studying his books, accompanying him on calls, preparing medicines, cultivating
the herb garden, tending the horses, et cetera. He usually
paid a substantial fee to his preceptor and often was one of
several apprentices serving at the same time.

The barber-surgeons, also known as bone-setters, were
likewise apprenticed to each other and sometimes it was a
family affair, father to son, and so on. They also did blood-
letting either at the request of a physician or an individual.
Blood-letting was considered to have tonic effects in well persons, especially in the spring of the year. Barber-surgeons
were called in most cases of severe trauma, fractures, dis-
locations and lacerations. In Seabury's later years he was

to become acquainted with a number of regular physicians
who had become surgeons as a result of an extended experience during the Revolution in the army hospitals and in the
field. They took over most of the work of the barber-surgeons, extending the field to include amputations, removal
of tumors, thyroid operations, opening the skull and other
major procedures. They did heroic surgery in every mean-
ing of the word.

The midwives had been an important part of the picture
from the beginning. Their tradition went back to Mayflower
days and a time when in England midwives were licenced by
the Bishop of London. A number of the colonial midwives
were so qualified. Here they did other things beside deliver
women. They cared for the sick as nurses, prescribed some
remedies and no doubt were called upon to give advice in
gynecologic disorders. In Seabury's day one of the most
celebrated midwives was Elizabeth Smithson of Guilford of
whom her famous son-in-law Jared Eliot said, "She knew
when to exert herself vigourously and also when it was her
strength to sit still."[1] Sound obstetrical acumen, if ever
there was.

But little is recorded of the nurse or "nursing mother".
Every community had women who nursed the sick. Often
they were widows and such a one was Agnes Pember of New
London who is described as a "nursing mother or doctress."[2]

She was said to be ready to mount her horse day or night at
a summons. Her services were in high demand for she was
something of a local celebrity. As with midwives these
nurses undoubtedly prescribed simple remedies and home
concoctions.

Many of the remedies used by physicians in Seabury's
time seem ridiculous, but, on the other hand, many of the
drugs prescribed were therapeutically sound, such as,
opium, laudanum, belladonna, ipecac, cinchona bark, (qui-
nine), mercury and the mineral salts. This is another side
to a picture usually obscured by the use of blood-letting for
almost all ills. To this other aspect should be added the
recognition of the importance of such things as warmth, rest,
good food, exercise, bathing, and general cleanliness. Isola-
tion was generally practised in contagious disease.

An aspect of medical practice in that day we must not
overlook is that of illnesses due to psychosomatic disorder,
a modern name covering manifestations of mental illness
which were as frequent then as now. If we question this we
should remind ourselves that Seabury's time was not too far
removed from the days of universal belief in witchcraft. The
Salem tragedies of 1692 were only 37 years previous to his
birth. If at his period the Puritan's belief in such evil spirits
had largely disappeared the horrific side of his religion still
remained. For him the fires of hell still burned fiercely for

the sinner in ways stimulating to the mind of the imaginative.

The cleric physician was surely in a position to deal suc-
cessfully with certain types of mental illness, hysteria, anx-
iety states, and the like. He knew the members of his flock
as did no one else, their family characteristics, idiosyncra-
sies. His advice in many of such illnesses would be considered as good psychotherapy today. We must remember
that the minister in colonial Connecticut was usually a man
well experienced in worldly affairs and was the arbiter of
most problems that appeared in his community, including
those of politics.

Just how the cleric physician actually functioned in medical practice we must conjecture. No doubt he was called in
most cases of serious illness. Minor illnesses were mostly
taken care of by members of some of the groups mentioned.
Aware of the cleric physicians educational background and
his social position these other practitioners would regard
his word with a good deal of finality. The cleric physicians
and the regular physicians recognised numerous contagious
diseases and some constitutional disorders for which standard treatment was to be found in medical books. And, we
must believe that the presence of the cleric physician in the
sick room had therapeutic values of its own.

It is in the Jamaica and Westchester years that we
should picture Seabury as a cleric physician. Both of these

communities were well settled and those of the healing arts
groups I have mentioned were to be found in proximity. It
is hard to imagine that anyone even among Seabury's parishioners considered him as being "on call" in the modern sense
of medical practice. He would have made regular calls on
the chronically ill of his parish and have responded to emer-
gency situations. Otherwise most of his medical visits would
be those of a consultative character giving to those who were
caring for the sick the benefit of his medical experience and
wisdom. On occasion he may have been called outside of his
parish. The famed Jared Eliot made such excursions to Newport and Boston. One thinks of Samuel Seabury as a man of
great faith in himself and in his earthly mission, faith to
serve his church as a good priest, his school as a good master, and his patients as a good physician. It was in recognition of this great attribute that his fellow clergy chose him
to become their bishop.

After becoming Bishop of Connecticut there is evidence
that Seabury kept an active interest in medical affairs. This
is seen in his endorsement of the celebrated "Cases and Observations", published by the Medical Society of New Haven
County in 1788, the first medical transactions published in
the New World. The medical historian Henry Bronson writes,
"Among those who complimented the work was the secretary
of the American Academy of Arts and Sciences, Boston, Dr.

John Warren, Boston, <u>Bishop Seabury</u>, the president of the
College of Physicians of Philadelphia, and Drs. John Morgan
and James Mease of the same place".[3]

In medical circles in 1788 the name of Bishop Seabury
meant something more than only that of an important church
dignitary.

Chapter Seven

THE QUEST FOR THE EPISCOPATE

The end of the war came in 1783 with a proclamation of peace being given to the American Army on the 19th of April exactly eight years from the day of the Battle of Lexington. The great question which now faced the American clergy of the English Church was what to do under the changed conditions. The final treaty of peace had taken no notice of their religious rights so it remained for the States to deal with them and the loyalists as they saw fit. Some of these, notably Massachusetts, New York and Virginia, adopted measures of great severity. In New York so much violence was threatened that Sir Guy Carleton wrote to the President of the Congress that the loyalists "conceived the safety of their lives depended upon his removing them elsewhere."[1] The only thing the Crown could do was to offer them safety in migration to Nova Scotia and other British territories. About twelve thousand men, women and children were said to have embarked from New York to Nova Scotia and the Bahamas, and many of the clergy went with them, the latter being given increased salaries from the Society and receiving grants of land.

Seabury had no desire to leave his native land but his parish in Westchester was so depleted and ruined that he

could not return to it. In Staten Island the conditions were
much the same. For the time being he remained in New
York supporting his family chiefly by his medical practice.

In Connecticut, as we have seen, conditions were more
favorable for the Church than in other northern states. The
clergy there, with the exception of John Beach of Newtown,
had been compelled to cease their prayers for the King and
royal family but were not much hampered otherwise as far
as the Liturgy was concerned. To their way of thinking they
needed more than ever a head or central authority before
proceeding to revise the Book of Common Prayer. While
the British Cabinet might acknowledge that an American
Episcopate might be a good thing, any action on the subject
was kept in abeyance. As far as the Americans were concerned, the jurisdiction of the Bishop of London which had
been inactive during the war, at its conclusion was abandoned.
Furthermore, the laws of England remained unchanged and
contained the oath of allegiance to the King at ordination
which obviously could not be taken by them even if they
journeyed to England for Orders. Unless bishops could be
had for the Church in the States, that Church by its own laws
could not perpetuate itself. Any change in the English law
depended upon civil rather than ecclesiastical authority, and
any sanction by the Parliament of an act to allow English
bishops to function in America might be interpreted as an

insult to the newly made independent States. Those and other
questions were very much in the minds of the Clergy in Connecticut. Their present duties they could perform with satis-
faction, but the future held no prospect for any continuance.
Nothing less than a bishop for the Church in Connecticut
would satisfy them although they recognised a common
problem between themselves and their brethren in the other
States.

Following the war there were fourteen Episcopal clergymen in Connecticut, and on the 25th of March in 1783 ten of
their number met in the small village of Woodbury in Litch-
field County at a house used as a glebe by the Rev. John Rutgers Marshall, Missionary of the Society and Rector of St.
Paul's there. No layman was present at the meeting which
was kept so secret that only clergymen knew about it. Just
who the men were is not known to this day. The Rev. Abraham Jarvis of Middletown was secretary but no minutes were
kept. However, something of what went on at that memorable
occasion has been described for us by the Rev. Daniel Fogg,
one of the number, in a letter written July, 14 that same
year at Pomfret and addressed to the Rev. Samuel Parker of
Boston:

"Dear Sir,

I wrote you a few lines 2d inst. by an uncertain convey-
ance in which I attempted to excuse myself by throwing the
blame upon you for not waiting for you till the time you

mentioned. I now plead guilty and beg your forgiveness. I
likewise mentioned that the Connecticut Clergy had done all
in their power respecting the matter you were anxious about
but they keep it a profound secret even from their most intimate friends of the Laity. The matter is this: After consulting the Clergy in New York how to keep up the succession
they unanimously agreed to send a person to England to be
consecrated Bishop for America and pitched upon Dr. Seabury as the most proper person for this purpose, who sailed
for England the beginning of last month, highly recommended
by all the Clergy in New York, Connecticut &c. And if he
succeeds he is to come out as missionary for New London
or some other vacant mission. And if they will not receive
him in Connecticut, or in any other of the States of America,
he is to go to Nova Scotia. Sir Guy (Carleton) highly approves
of the plan and has used all his influence to favour it.

The Clergy have even gone so far as to instruct Dr. Seabury, if none of the regular Bishops of the Church of England
will ordain him, to go down to Scotland and receive ordination
from a nonjuring Bishop.

Please let me know by Mr. Grosvenor how you approve
of the plan and whether you have received any late accounts
from England.

From your affct. brother

D. Fogg"[2]

The Rev. Samuel Parker was a prominent Churchman in Bos-

ton and greatly interested in a better organization and estab-

lishment of the Church in this country. He believed with

others that Connecticut was then the most favorable state in

which to establish a see. Within two weeks he received

another letter from Daniel Fogg assuring him that he and

his brothers in Massachusetts would not come under Seabury's jurisdiction if they did not care to do so. "I am very glad," wrote Fogg," the conduct of the Connecticut Clergy meets with your approbation in the main ... as to the objection of not consulting the clergy of the other States, the time would not allow of it, and there was nobody to consult in the State of New York, for there is not one clergyman there except refugees, and they were consulted ... . And in your State and New Hampshire, you know how many there are, and you know there is no compulsion in the matter, and you will be left to act as you please, either to be subject to him or not."[3]

The selection of Seabury at Woodbury in one sense was not an election in conformity to Church usage. W. J. Seabury speaks of it rather as a "designation", that is, it was not an election by Dean and Chapter nor by a body of delegates appointed by incorporated parishes. It was an election, nevertheless. The Connecticut Churchmen in the urgency of the situation did what was only possible for them to do, revert to general principles recognised by the Church before the adoption of special rules. Within the Church there exists a distinction between Order and Jurisdiction, the former being the power to execute the function of the ministry and the latter the lawful right to exercise that power. Thus when Bishop Seabury's jurisdiction was established, all things necessary were concurred. He was consecrated for his

particular district by Bishops, he was chosen by the Clergy
before his consecration, received wholeheartedly by the
Church Laity of his district and his residence there sanctioned
by civil authority. It is interesting that the pattern set by
Connecticut of a church complete in itself as a district was
that subsequently followed in the other States.

Seabury arrived in London on July 7, 1783. Here for a
year and a half he was destined to remain at his own expense,
planning his moves, and cooling his heels in seemingly end-
less waiting for a decision which would enable the British
bishops to act in his behalf. For a man of his temperament
it must have been a trying and discouraging time. The chief
record we have of his sojourn in Great Britain are his letters
to fellow clergy in America and they are splendid. His adroit-
ness in expression reveals his astuteness in managing his
great affair and clearly shows that the little group at Woodbury had without question "pitched upon" the right man for a
difficult and arduous job.

The first letter, dated July 15, a week after landing is
addressed to those who elected him. Having failed of an in-
terview with the Archbishop of York who had left London, Seabury had waited upon the Bishop of London and there received
a cordial reception. "He heartily approved," he writes, "of
the scheme and wished success to it, and declared his read-
iness to concur with the two Archbishops in carrying it into

execution: but I soon found out he was not disposed to take a lead in the matter. He mentioned the State Oaths in the Ordination offices, as impediments, but supposed the King's dispensation would be sufficient warrant for the Archbishops to proceed upon. But on conversing with His Grace of Canterbury, I found his opinion rather different from the Bishop of London. He received me politely, approved of the measure, saw the necessity of it and would do all he could to carry it into execution. But he must proceed openly and with candor. His Majesty's dispensation he feared, would not be sufficient to justify the omission of oaths imposed by act of Parliament. He would consult the other Bishops; he would advise with those persons on whose judgment he thought he could depend. He was glad to hear the opinion of the Bishop of London, and wished to know the sentiments of the Archbishop of York. He foresaw great difficulties, but hoped there were none of them insurmountable."[4]

On the 10th of the next month he reports his visit to the Archbishop of York. "This journey," he writes, "I have accomplished, and I fear to very little purpose. His Grace is now carrying on a correspondence with the Archbishop of Canterbury on the subject; what the issue will be is not certain; but I think unless matters can be put on a different footing, the business will not succeed. Both the Archbishops are convinced of the necessity of supplying the States of

America with Bishops, if it be intended to preserve the
Episcopal Church there; and they even seem sensible of the
justice of the present application, but they are exceedingly
embarrassed by the following difficulties: (1) That it would
be sending a bishop to Connecticut, which they have no right
to do without the consent of the State. (2) That the bishop
would not be received in Connecticut. (3) That there would
be no adequate support for him. (4) That the oaths in the
ordination office cannot be got over, because the king's dispensation would not be sufficient to justify the omission of
those oaths. At least there must be the concurrence of the
king's council to the omission; and that the council would not
give their concurrence without the permission of the State of
Connecticut to the bishop's residing among them.

All I could say had no effect, and I had a fair opportunity
of saying all that I wished to say. It now remains to be considered what method shall be taken to obtain the wished-for
Episcopate.

The matter here will become public. It will soon get to
Connecticut. Had you not, gentlemen, better make immed-
iate application to the State for permission to have a bishop
reside there? Should you not succeed, you lose nothing, as
I am pretty confident you will not succeed here without such
consent. Should there be anything personal with regard to
me, let it not retard the matter. I will most readily give

up my pretensions to any person who will be agreeable to
you, and less exceptionable to the State."[5]

On September 3rd, 1783 Seabury wrote to his friend
Jeremiah Leaming, "With regard to my success I do not only
think it doubtful, but that the probaility is against it. Nobody
here will risk anything for the sake of the Church, or for the
sake of continuing Episcopal ordination in America. Unless
therefore it can be made a ministerial affair, none of the
bishops will proceed in it for fear of clamor; and indeed the
ground on which they at present stand, seems to me so uncertain, that I believe they are obliged to take great care
with regard to any step they take out of the common road.
They are apprehensive that my consecration would be looked
on in the light of sending a bishop to Connecticut, and that the
State of Connecticut would resist it, and that they should be
censored as meddlers in matters which do not concern them.
This is the great reason why I wish that the State of Connecticut should be applied to for their consent. Without it, I
think nothing will be done. If they refuse, the whole matter
is at an end. If they consent that a bishop should reside
among them, the grand obstacle will be removed. You see
the necessity of making the attempt, and of making it with
vigor. One reason, indeed, why I wish the attempt to be
made in Connecticut, related to myself. I cannot continue
here long: necessity will oblige me to leave it in March or

April, at furthest. If this business fails, I must try to get
some provision made for myself: and indeed the State of
Connecticut may consent that a bishop should reside among
them, though they might not consent that I should be the man.
In that case, I beg that no clergyman in Connecticut will hesitate a moment on my account. The point is, to get the Episcopal authority into that country; and he shall have every assistance in my power ... . Dr. Chandler's appointment to
Nova Scotia will, I believe succeed. And possibly he may
go there this autumn, or at least early in the spring. But
his success will do no good in the States of America. His
hand will be as much tied as the bishops in England; and I
think he will run no risks to communicate the Episcopal powers. There is, therefore, everything depending on the success of the application to the State of Connecticut. It must
be made quickly, lest the dissenters here should interpose
and prevent it; and it should be made with the united efforts
of clergy and laity, that its weight may be greater; and its
issue you must make me acquainted with as soon as you can."[6]

The impression which Seabury seems to have received
from the archbishops was that there might be a concurrence
of the King's Council in dispensing with the obligation to take
the oath of allegiance, if the State of Connecticut would give
permission for a bishop to reside there. His insistent letters on this subject finally aroused the Connecticut Clergy to

take action and meet in Wallingford in convention where they
appointed Leaming, Jarvis and Hubbard to meet with leading
members of both Houses of the Assembly then sitting in New
Haven. In a letter from these brethren to Seabury, dated
February 5, 1784 the report of this conference was made.
"Your right," they said, "is unquestionable. You therefore
have our full concurrence for your enjoyment of your own
ecclesiastical constitution, we would freely give our votes
for such an act. We have passed a law which embraces your
Church, wherein are comprehended all the legal rights and
powers, intended by our Constitution to be given to any denomination of Christians. In that act is included all that you
want ... . The introduction of a bishop on the present footing, without anything more, in their opinion would be the
easiest and securest way in which it could be done, and we
might be sure of his protection. This they thought must be
enough to satisfy the bishops, and all concerned in the affair
in England ... .

"The act above alluded to, you will receive in a letter
from Mr. Leaming, attested by the clerk of the lower House
of Assembly. It is not yet published. The clerk was so
obliging as to copy it from the journals of the House. You
were mentioned as the gentleman we had pitched upon. The
Secretary of State, from personal knowledge, and others,
said things honorable and benevolent towards you. Now if

the opinion of the Governor and other members of the council, explicitly given in entire agreement with the most respectable members among the representatives, who must be
competent judges of their own civil polity, is reasonable sufficient to remove all scruples about the concurrence of the
legislature, we cannot imagine that objection will any longer
have a place in the minds of the Archbishops."[8]

The act passed by the Connecticut legislature was entitled, "An Act for securing the rights of conscience in matters of Religion to Christians of every denomination in this
State." By its provisions no persons professing the Christian
religion who, —" soberly and conscientiously dissent from the
worship and ministry by Law established in the Society wherein they dwell, and attend public worship by themselves, shall
incur any penalty for not attending the worship and ministry
so established.... That all denominations of Christians
differing in their religious sentiments from the people of the
Established Societies in this State, whether the Episcopal
Church, or those Congregationalists called Separates, or the
people called Baptists, or Quakers, or any other denomination who shall have formed into distinct churches or congregations, and attend public worship, and support the Gospel
Ministry in a way agreeable to their consciences and respective professions ... every such person shall be exempted
from being taxed for the support of the worship and Ministry

of Said Society, so long as he or they shall continue to so attend and support public worship with a different Church or Congregation as aforesaid."[8]

The chief support for maintaining a bishop is found in the following provision which reads, "all such Protestant Churches and Congregations ... shall have the liberty and authority to use and exercise the same powers of maintaining and supporting their respective ministers ... as the Ecclesiastical Societies ... ."[8]

However plain that was, the Archbishop of Canterbury, under the guidance of the ministry, was able to discover new objections to the consecration. These are summarized for us in a memorandum made by Seabury on the back of a letter to Myles Cooper, (August 31, 1784.) It reads,— "Objections made to the Connecticut Episcopate by the British Ministry, as represented to Dr. Seabury by his Grace of Cant. the beginning of Aug[t]. 1784.

1. That they cannot consent that a Bp. be consecrated for Connecticut, till the N. Scotia Episcopate be settled.

2. Nor unless Congress requested, or, at least acquiesced in the measure.

3. That Conn[t]. was only one State and even their consent was not explicitly declared.

4. That the application was only from the Clergy and not from the laity in Conn[t].

5. That the Laity of the Episcopal Communion in America were adverse to the having Bps. resident among them.

6. That the Country was not divided into Dioceses, nor
any provision made for Bps.

7. That never having sent Bps. into America while the
13 States were subject to Great Britain, it would have a very
suspicious look to do it now, and would probably create, or
augment, ill will in that Country against G. B."[9]

On the 17th of June 1784 Seabury received a copy of the
act of the Connecticut legislature from Josiah Leaming and
ten days later he wrote to Abraham Jarvis at Middletown, "I
have had a long conversation with the Archbishop of Canterbury, and another with the Archbishop of York on the act.
They seem to think the principal objections are removed as
far as you and I are concerned. They spoke handsomely of
the Clergy of Connecticut, and declared themselves satisfied
with your humble servant, whom the Clergy were pleased to
recommend to them but I apprehend there are some difficulties that may not easily be got over. These arise from the re-
strictions the Bishops are under about consecrating without
the King's leave, and the doubt seems to be about the King's
leave to consecrate a Bishop who is not to reside in his do-
minions; and about the validity of his dispensing with the oath
in case he has the power to grant leave of consecration. I
have declared my opinion, which is, that as there is no law

existing relative to a Bishop who is to reside in a foreign
State, the Archbishops are left to the general laws of The
Christian Church, and have no need either of the King's
leave or dispensation. But the opinion of so little a man cannot have much weight ... . Believe me there is nothing I
have so much at heart as the accomplishment of the business
you have intrusted to my management; and I am ready to
make every sacrifice of worldly consideration that may stand
in the way of its completion."[10]

By the middle of the year 1784, Seabury had been in England for more than a year and however kindly the English
Bishops might feel toward him and his undertaking they did
not think it legal to grant his request unless an act of Parliament should authorize them to do so. That body did finally
get into action in Church matters by passing an act authoriz-
ing the Bishop of London and his substitutes to dispense with
the oaths which precluded ordination of foreign candidates for
the diaconate and the priesthood; but without the admission
of candidates for the Episcopate to the same privilege. As
far as Seabury's quest was concerned he was hardly better
off than he was the day he arrived in London. It now became
necessary for him to look elsewhere.

The choice that confronted him was to seek consecration
through the non juring succession of the Scottish Church or by
certain non juring bishops in the line of Sancroft then residing

in England. The latter succession, as did the former, dated
from the time of William and Mary had ascended the throne
and demanded the allegiance of all the bishops. Sancroft,
Archbishop of Canterbury, and six other of the English bishops refused to take any new oath on the ground that they had
already taken such an oath to James II and could not forswear
themselves. The non jurors as they were called were de-
prived of their sees and were looked upon as separatists.
This division went on for a considerable time but finally lost
momentum and disappeared. In Seabury's time there still
lived a few of the English non juring bishops and two of them,
Bishops Cartwright and Price were willing to consecrate him,
an offer which he refused on the ground that he had already
applied to Scotland.

The case of the Scottish non jurors was different. They
were not separatists from the body of a National Episcopate
but part of the whole body itself. There had been no schism
in that church, for all of it had been cast out of royal favor
at one time. With King William it was either a recognition
of the Presbyterians as constituting the national Scottish
Church or the Episcopalians. He chose the former. His
first Parliament abolished the Scottish Episcopal jurisdiction
and severe persecution followed.

Thus it was that the Scottish bishops occupied a position
of their own. They were part of a national and independent

church with no other Episcopate opposing them. Their Episcopate was located in a country never previously occupied by
any other line of bishops and it had operated with the concur-
rent consent of the clergy and the people over whom it was
exercised. The Scottish bishops took the stand that if the
absence of civil authority was a defect of jurisdiction then it
was no different than the defect which existed in the jurisdiction of the Apostles and their successors in the Primitive
Church. They maintained that their Order and Jurisdiction
was that by Divine Authority of the Episcopate and independent
of any sanction of civil power.

Months before Seabury had been forced to his decision
in London, the way in Scotland had been opened for him. In
October 1782, before Seabury had even left his own country,
the Rev. Dr. George Berkeley, second son of Bishop Berkeley,
Yale's great benefactor, had written to Bishop John Skinner
of Aberdeen, Coadjutor of Bishop Robert Kilgour, expressing
the hope that, "a most important good might erelong be derived to the nearly neglected sons of Protestant Episcopacy
on the other side of the Atlantic from the suffering Church
of Scotland ... and I would humbly submit it, to the bishops
of the Church in Scotland (as we style her in Oxford) whether
this be not the time peculiarly favorable to the introduction
of the Protestant Episcopate on the footing of universal toleration, and before any anti-Episcopal establishment shall have
taken place."[11]

Berkeley followed with another letter, saying, "Had my honored father's scheme for planting an Episcopal college, whereof he was to be president, in the Summer Islands (The Bahamas) not been sacrificed by the worst minister that Britain ever saw, probably under a mild monarch (who loves the Church of England as much as I believe his grandfather hated it), Episcopacy would have been established in America by a succession from the English Church, unattended by any invidious temporal rank or power. But the dissenting miscellaneous interest in England has watched with too successful a jealousy, over the honest intentions of our best bishops ... . From the Churches of England and Ireland, America will not now receive the Episcopate; if she might, I am persuaded that many of her sons would joyfully receive bishops from Scotland. The question then, shortly is, can any proper persons be found who, with the spirit of confessors, would convey the great blessing of the Protestant Episcopacy from the persecuted Church of Scotland to the struggling persecuted Protestant Episcopal worshippers in America."[12]

Bishop John Skinner was without doubt sympathetic to Berkeley's plea but he saw difficulties in the way and said so in his reply,— "Nothing can be done with safety on our side, till the independence of America be fully and irrevocably recognised by the government of Britain; and even then the enemies of the Church might make a handle of our correspondence

with the colonies as a proof that we always wished to fish in
troubled waters, and we have little need to give ground for
an implication of this kind."[13]

It seems likely that Seabury's arrival and mission in
England in July 1783 was known in Scotland for some time.
But, it was not until November of that year that a letter was
written by Mr. Elphinstone, the son of a Scottish clergyman
to Robert Kilgour, the Primus or presiding Bishop of the
Church of Scotland. That interested layman asked the prelate, "Can consideration be obtained for an already dignified
and well-vouched American clergyman, now at London, for
the purpose of perpetuating the Episcopal Reformed Church
in America, particularly in Connecticut?"[14]

About this same time Berkeley again wrote to Bishop
Skinner saying, "I have this day heard, I need not add with
the sincerest pleasure that a respectable presbyter, well
recommended from America, has arrived in London, seeking
what it seems, in the present state of affairs, he cannot expect to receive in our Church. Sure, dear Sir, the Scotch
prelates, who are not shackled by any Erastian Connection,
(State supremacy in ecclesiastical affairs), will not send
this suppliant empty away. I scruple not to give it as my decided opinion that the king, some of his counsellors, all our
bishops, (except, peradventure, the Bishop of St. Alsaph),
and all the learned and respectable clergy of our Church,

will at least secretely rejoice, if a Protestant bishop, be
sent from Scotland to America; but more especially if Connecticut be the scene of his ministry."[15]

On the 26th of June, 1784, Seabury wrote to Abraham
Jarvis of the Connecticut Committee, "I have had some opportunities of consulting some very respectable clergymen
in this matter, and their invariable opinion, is that should I,
be disappointed here, where the business had been so fairly,
candidly and honorably pursued, it would become my duty to
obtain Episcopal consecration whereever it can be had, and
that no exception could be taken here at my doing so. The
Scotch succession was named. It was said to be equal to any
succession in the world, etc. There I know consecration may
be had. But with regard to this matter I hope to hear from
you in answer to a letter I wrote to Mr. Leaming, I think in
April. Should I receive any instructions from the Clergy of
Connecticut, I shall attend to them, if not, I shall act according to the best advice I can get, and my own judgment."[16]

From that letter and others it appears that Seabury had
some concern about going to Scotland for consecration. The
first concern was the reaction, whether favorable or not, to
the Scottish succession not only in Connecticut but in the other
colonies. He was anxious not to offend the dignitaries in the
English Church some of whom had listened to him so sympa-
thetically. He was also anxious not to offend the Society from

which he and other Americans were still collecting salaries.
He surmised that the Scottish Bishops might think that he was
adopting a superior attitude. Lastly, and of high importance,
his money was running out.

A month after writing to Abraham Jarvis he again addressed the Clergy of Connecticut to assure himself again of
their backing, a caution which at first sight seems paradox-
ical in a man of his nature. Nevertheless, the gravity of the
move was very real now that the time for decision had come.
"If nothing can be done," he wrote, "I shall give up the matter here as unattainable, and apply to the North, unless I
should receive contrary directions from the Clergy of Connecticut. The various difficulties I have had to struggle with,
and the various steps I have taken to get through them, are
too long to enumerate by letter; but I hope to spend the next
winter in Connecticut, and then you shall know all, at least
all that I shall remember."[17]

On August 31, 1784 Seabury wrote to Myles Cooper, then
at Edinburgh, telling him of the act passed by the Connecticut
legislature enabling Episcopal congregations to transact their
ecclesiastical affairs on their own principles, adding that.,
"The Legislature of Connecticut know that a Bishop is applied for, they know the person in whose favour the application is made, and they give no opposition to either .... On
this ground it is that I apply to the good Bishops of Scotland.

If they consent to impart the Episcopal succession to the
Church of Connecticut, they will, I think, do a good work and
the blessings of thousands will attend them ... . I indeed
think it my duty to conduct the matter in such a manner as
shall risk the salaries which the Missionaries in Connecticut
receive from the Society here as little as possible; and I persuade myself it may be done, so as to make that risk next to
nothing. With respect to my own salary—if the Society
choose to withdraw it, I am ready to part with it ... . I am
anxious to return to America this autumn, and the winter is
fast approaching, when the voyage will be attended with double inconvenience and danger, and the expense of continuing
here another winter is greater than will suit my purse."[18]

W. J. Seabury records a note from Myles Cooper to
Bishop Kilgour which reads, "Dr. Cooper presents his most
respectful compliments to Bishop Kilgour, and begs leave to
acquaint him, that to Dr. Cooper's knowledge, Dr. Seabury
is recommended by several worthy clergymen in Connecticut
as a person worthy of promotion, and to whom they are willing to submit as a bishop. Dated Edin[h]. 13th September 1784.
Postscript by another hand.—Dr. Berkeley, in consequence of
some fears suggested by Bp. Skinner, wrote the present
Archbishop of Canterbury, that application had been made by
Seabury to the Scottish Bishops for consecration, and begged,
that if his grace thought the Bishops here run any hazard in

complying with Dr. Seabury's request, he would be so good
as (to) give Dr. Berkeley notice immediately, but his Grace
was satisfied there was no danger, there was no occasion to
give any answer. No answer came."[19]

The fears expressed by Bishop Skinner through Berkeley show again the tight situation of the Scottish Church. Although the harshness of the old laws had been somewhat
blunted, yet in the mind of that prelate any new grievance
might fan remaining embers of persecution into flame. At
the time Bishop Skinner was obliged to make provision for
his small flock in the upper two stories of his own house located in an obscure part of Aberdeen, called Longacre.

Actually things were moving favorably for Seabury in
the fall of 1784. On the 2nd of October, Bishop Kilgour wrote
to Rev. John Allen of Edinburgh that he had heard from Seabury and that the Scottish Bishops were "still waiting to comply with his purpose; to cloathe him with the Episcopal character, and thereby convey to the Western World the blessing
of a free, valid and purely ecclesiastical Episcopacy ... .
We are concerned that he should have been so long in deter-
mining himself to make this application and wish that in an
affair of so much importance that he had corresponded with
one of our number. However, as he appears open and candid
on his part; he may believe the Bishops will be no less so on
their part; and will be glad how soon he can set out for the
North."[20]

The Bishop's letter to Allen was communicated to Seabury who, as may be imagined, was anxious to say something for himself regarding the obvious innuendo. On the 14th
of October he wrote to Bishop Kilgour from London; "Three
days ago I was made happy by the receipt of a letter from my
friend in Edinburgh, enclosing one from you to the Rev[d]. Mr.
John Allen signifying the consent of the Bishops in Scotland
to convey through me the blessing of a free, valid and purely
ecclesiastical Episcopacy to the Western World, etc. ... .
Whatever appearance there may have been of inattention on
my part they (the Bishops) will I trust, when I shall have the
happiness of a personal appearance, be fully, and to a mind
so candid and liberal as yours, satisfactorily explained. I
propose through the favour of God's good providence to be at
Aberdeen by the 10th of November, and there shall wait the
conveniency of the Bishops who have so humanely taken this
matter under their management."[21]

At this period the Scottish Church had four bishops,
Robert Kilgour, Bishop of Aberdeen and Primus, Arthur
Petrie, Bishop of Ross and Moray, Charles Rose, Bishop of
Dunblane, and John Skinner, Coadjutor Bishop of Aberdeen.
From here on it was plain sailing for Seabury at Aberdeen
but there had been efforts to influence the bishops there from
consecrating him. One such was a letter from Rev. William
Smith, a Scot by birth who was at the time head of the Wash-

ington College in Maryland. He alleged that any such consecration was against the advice of the Archbishops of Canterbury and York and that these prelates did not consider the
candidate a fit person because of his activities against Congress. He also said the people of America were not ready
for such a step. Beardsley maintains that Smith, "had views
of his own to promote, and hoped and made efforts to be
raised to the Episcopate in Maryland."[22] The source of his
information about the opinion of the archbishops was likely
gossip but no doubt in some quarters in America the "Westchester Farmer" was thought to be something less than the
ideal candidate for the first American Episcopate.

It should be recorded that, at a later date, friendly relations were established between Bishop Seabury and Dr. Smith
and the latter did useful work in promoting the interests of
the Church in organizing dioceses in America. Another op-
ponent to the consecration came ex post facto in a personal
attack on Bishop Seabury by Mr. Granville Sharp, a grandson
of Dr. John Sharp, sometime Archbishop of York. He wrote
to the Archbishop of Canterbury crying down the non juring
Bishops of Scotland and saying that Seabury proposed to go
to America to obtain jurisdiction over several congregations
in Connecticut.

Granville Sharp's chief interest in discrediting the Scottish consecration was due to his disappointment in the act

which limited holy orders to the ordination of deacons and priests. Afterwards Sharp used his good offices to the end that Episcopacy should be obtained from the English bishops. Three years after Seabury's consecration at Aberdeen that actually happened at Lambeth Palace in the consecration of Samuel Provoost as Bishop of New York, and William White, as Bishop of Pennsylvania, February 4, 1787.

Chapter Eight

THE CONNECTICUT EPISCOPATE

On Sunday morning, November 14, 1784, the Rev. Samuel Seabury, D.D. was elevated to the high order of the Episcopate by the laying on of hands investing him "with proper powers for governing all Episcopal offices in the Church in Connecticut." The ceremony was performed by Bishop Robert Kilgour, Primus, assisted by Bishops Arthur Petrie and John Skinner, "in the presence of a considerable number of respectable clergymen and a great number of laity." But, the chapel in the upper floor of John Skinner's house was a far cry from Lambeth Palace, a circumstance in the minds of the Bishops who next day wrote to the Clergy in Connecticut: "In the discharge of this duty, the example we wish to copy after is that of the Primitive Church while in a similar situation, unconnected with and unsupported by the temporal powers."[1]

Following the sermon the last four verses of the ninetieth psalm in the new version of Tate and Bradley were sung. The words were appropriate to the suppression of the Church in Scotland and her struggles in the new western democracy.

> "To satisfy and cheer our souls,
>   The early mercy send;
> That we may all our days to come
>   In joy and comfort spend.

Let happy times, with large amends,
   Dry up our former tears,
Or equal, at the least, the term
   Of our afflicted years.

To all our servants, Lord, let this
   Thy wondrous work be known;
And to our offspring yet unborn,
   Thy glorious power be shown.

Let thy bright rays upon us shine,
   Give thou our work success;
The glorious work we have in hand,
   Do thou vouchsafe to bless."[2]

In the same upper room in the afternoon of the day of his consecration, Bishop Seabury preached. The earnestness of his words and his delivery of them were impressive to a Scottish audience not used to much animation in their pulpits. The Church historian Grub in a letter written in 1879 records, "My father, then a boy, was present, and has often spoken to me about it. He recollected particularly that the bishop used more gesture than was common in Scotland, and that he waved a white handkerchief as he preached."[3]

The following day the Bishop and his Consecrators signed a Concordat or Bond of Union "between the Catholic remainder of the ancient Church of Scotland, and the now rising Church in the State of Connecticut," in which among other things they declared that; "As the Celebration of the Holy Eucharist ... is the principle Bond of Union among Christians, as well as the most solemn Act of Worship in the Christian Church,"

they, the signers, desired to keep the Liturgy of the new
Church in America as close as possible to that of Scotland.
The Scottish Bishops, "Tho'... very far from prescribing to
their Brethren in this matter," urged Bishop Seabury to "en-
deavor all he can consistently with peace and prudence, to
make the Celebration of this venerable Mystery conformable
to the most primitive Doctrine and Practice ... which is the
pattern the Church of Scotland has copied after her Communion Office, and which it has been the Wish of some of the most
eminent Divines of the Church of England, that she also had
more closely followed than she seems to have done since she
gave up her first reformed Liturgy used in the Reign of King
Edward VI."[4]

At a later date Bishop Seabury was able to persuade the
American Church to follow the Scottish Communion Office in
its Prayer Book of 1789, now regarded by liturgical scholars
as superior to that of the 1662 English Prayer Book.

At the time of his consecration at Aberdeen, Samuel
Seabury was 56 years old with his most important life work
still ahead, a task which would require the utmost in vision,
clear thinking, energy and tact. In full maturity he seems to
have had all of those attributes. From his long period of
waiting in London, month after month with little happening,
we must acknowledge that he had ample opportunity to learn,
in the words of the Rev. Jared Eliot, "when it was his
strength to sit still."[5]

Samuel Seabury seems to have had an early sense of
mission in life which never wavered. William Seabury, so
familiar with his journals, from these sources writes, "There
is always evidence of his abiding consciousness that he was
not his own, but that he belonged wholly to God, in whose
presence, and under whose fatherly protection, he lived,
moved and had his being. Such habitual devotion, and the
utter simplicity of the faith and love out of which it grew, be-
long to a type of Christian character which the world knows
little of, and which the Church, one is sometimes tempted
to think, has well nigh forgotten. But it has existed, and
doubtless still does exist; though to describe it now would be
but describing the fashion of a kind of life which some of us
can well remember to have been brought up in, but which few,
alas, can be conscious of having continued to keep ... no account of the Bishop's life would be complete without the recognition of the characteristics which have been noted, and of
which the Journal and other records afford so much evidence.
Yet it is not to be inferred that these characteristics at all
obscured the cheerfulness and brightness of temper and de-
meanor which were natural to him. Quite the contrary seems
to have been the case; and there are many stories which show
the easy, kindly and agreeable conversational habit which he
had; and the keen perseption of humor, and quick flashes of
wit by which his conversation was enlivened."[6]

Going back to the consecration and the events which followed, we learn that the sermon which Bishop John Skinner
preached on that occasion attracted considerable attention in
London where we can be sure some ears were being held to
the ground. In his discourse the Bishop spoke feelingly of
the position which he and his colleagues were in, saying, "As
long as there are nations to be instructed in the principles of
one gospel, or a Church to be formed in any part of the inhab-
ited world, the successors of the Apostles are obliged by the
commission which they hold, to contribute, as far as they
can, or may be required of them, to the propagation of those
principles, and to the formation of every Church, upon the
most pure and primitive model. No fear of wordly censure
ought to keep them back from so good a work; no connection
with any state, nor dependence on any government whatever
should tie their hands from communicating the blessing of
that kingdom which is not of this world, and diffusing the
means of salvation by a valid and regular ministry, whereever they may be wanted."[7]

The most important critic of Bishop Skinner's sermon
was said to be no less than Bishop Lowth of London, who addressed a letter to Bishop Kilgour signed as from "A Dignified Clergyman of the Church of England." His chief concern
seems to have been the harm that might come to the Church
in Scotland, saying, "Many of our Clergy have regarded as

hardly dealth with, and wished for a repeal of those laws
under which she now suffers. I have good reason to believe
that there is an intention formed of endeavoring to do her
some service at a convenient season; and I sincerely hope no
circumstance will intervene to frustrate that intention. It
pains me to say, however, that this sermon is not likely to
promote it. ..."[8]

The new Bishop did not remain at Aberdeen more than a
day or two but proceeded to London to make preparations for
the long journey home. In that place, as might be expected,
were some in high authority who did not take a favorable view
of the recent happenings in Aberdeen. Even Dr. Berkeley
who months before had paved the way for Seabury was not
satisfied with some of the documents signed there. The Bishop was aware of some of this adverse sentiment and spoke of
it in a letter dated January 5, 1785 addressed to the Rev.
Messrs. Leaming, Jarvis and Hubbard back in Connecticut.
Of Aberdeen, he writes, "It was the most solemn day I ever
passed: God grant that I may never forget it! I now only wait
for a good ship in which to return. None will sail before the
last of February or the first of March. The ship Triumph,
Capt. Stout, will be among the first. With this same Stout,
commander, and in the Triumph I expect to embark and hope
to be in New York some time in April. ... You will be
pleased to consider whether New London be the proper place

for me to reside at; or whether some other place would do better. At New London, however, I suppose they make some dependence on me. This ought to be taken into consideration. If I settle at New London, I must have an assistant. Look out, then, for some good clever young man who will go immediately into deacon's orders, and who would be willing to be with me in that capacity . . . . Since my return from Scotland, I have seen none of the Bishops but I have been informed that the step I have taken has displeased the two Archbishops, and it is now a matter of doubt whether I shall be continued on the Society's list . . . . My own poverty is one of the greatest discouragements I have. Two years absence from my family, and expensive residence here, has more than expended all I had. But in so good a cause, and of such magnitude, something must be risked by somebody. To my lot it had fallen; and I have done it cheerfully, and despair not of a happy issue."[9]

Among the American loyalists in London who had been helped to Seabury was the Rev. Jacob Duché of Philadelphia. During this present stay in London, Seabury met his son Thomas Spence Duché an artist who had been a pupil of Benjamin West. Seabury is said to have sat for his portrait at this time and the finishing touches are said to have been made by West. It was engraved by the noted engraver William Sharpe and is one of his finest. The Duché portrait of

Bishop Seabury is now preserved at Trinity College, Hartford,
and a copy made by Mildred Jordan in 1907 was presented
to Yale University by the late George Dudley Seymour.

During his final stay in London Bishop Seabury took steps
to preserve his status with the Society but it proved to be a
lost cause. In a letter to the Secretary, Seabury recounted
his mission to Britain in detail and the circumstances which
caused him to go to Scotland for his consecration. He made
a touching appeal for the Society's continued support and
wrote, "The fate of individuals is, however, of inferior moment when compared to that of the whole Church. Whenever
the Society shall wholly cease to interest itself in the con-
cerns of religion in America it will be a heavy calamity to
the Church in that Country."[10]

On his return to the Western World Seabury first landed
at Halifax where as Bishop he preached his first sermon in
America. He also visited his brother who had settled with
the loyalists in the Annapolis Valley. Within a few days of
landing he embarked from St. John for Newport Rhode Island
arriving there June 20, 1785. On the following Sunday he
preached his first sermon in the United States at Trinity
Church where a half century previous Dean Berkeley had
many times preached as an Episcopal clergyman. The next
day he left for New London reaching there on June 27th. All
in all, his journey home had taken three months.

The consecration of Bishop Seabury although a triumph
for the Church in America was something of a blow to the
English Church. About the time of the event John Adams was
in correspondence with the Danish Government with reference
to the ordination of an American student of divinity named
Mason Weems. A favorable answer from Copenhagen was
secured and the fact became known to the English Church
authorities, who paved the way for the ordination of Weems
in England. His Majesty, the King of Denmark informed Mr.
Adams that not only was ordination possible in Denmark but
that he was willing to set up a bishopric in one of the West
Indian Islands belonging to Denmark where candidates for
orders might go and thus save themselves of a lengthy and
costly voyage to Europe. It was the latter announcement
which brought matters to a head in England. In the Spring
session of the House of Lords in 1786 a statute was passed
allowing the Oath of Allegiance to be omitted at the consecration of bishops who were citizens of foreign countries. As
we have noted, in February of the next year, two American
clergymen, Provoost and White were consecrated in the
chapel of Lambeth Palace by the Archbishop of Canterbury.

Chapter Nine

BISHOP OF CONNECTICUT AND RHODE ISLAND

It is not the purpose of this memoir of Samuel Seabury to carry the story in detail through the years of his Episcopate from 1785 until his death eleven years later. His first official act after assuming his duties at New London was a meeting with the Episcopal clergy of Connecticut who had elected him and pledged their acceptance of him as their Bishop. Accordingly they met at Middletown on the 2nd of August 1785 with eleven of their numbers present as members of the convention. The Rev. Benjamin Moore of New York and the Rev. Samuel Parker of Boston had honorary seats in the meeting. Jeremiah Leaming was chosen president as usual and Abraham Jarvis as secretary. On the following day Bishop Seabury was formally received, greeted and accepted by his clergy. At this time the first ordination was held and four young men were made deacons. At eleven in the morning of August 4th divine service was held in the church, Mr. Parker read prayers and Mr. Moore presented a sermon after which Bishop Seabury delivered his first charge to the clergy. A passage from this message which deals with recommendations for Holy Orders expresses the view of what the Bishop felt the Church needed for sound growth. It also tells much of the ideals he held for himself,—

"Another matter which my duty requires me to mention, relates to a business in which you will probably be soon called upon to act. I mean the very important one of giving recommendations to candidates for Holy Orders. It is impossible that the Bishop should be personally acquainted with every one who may present himself for Ordination. He must, therefore, depend on the recommendation of his clergy and other people of reputation, for the character and qualifications of those who shall be presented to him. By qualifications, I mean not so much literary accomplishments, though these are not to be neglected, as aptitude for the work of the ministry. You must be sensible that a man may have, and deservedly have, an irreproachable moral character, and be endued with pious and devout affections, and a competent share of human learning, and yet from want of prudence, or from a deficiency in temper, or some singularity in disposition, may not be calculated to make a good clergyman; for to be a good clergyman, implies, among other things, that a man be a useful one. A clergyman who does no good always does hurt. There is no medium. Not only the moral character and learning and abilities of candidates are to be exactly inquired into, but also their good temper, prudence, diligence, and everything by which their usefulness in the ministry may be affected. Nor should their personal appearance, voice, manner, clearness of expression, and facility of communicating their sentiments, be overlooked. These, which may by some be thought to be only secondary qualifications, and therefore of no great importance, are, however, those that will require your more particular attention, and call for all your prudence. They who shall apply for recommendations, will generally be such as have passed through a course of academical studies, and must be competently qualified in a literary view."[1]

The second convocation met in New Haven according to adjournment on September 14, 1785 while Yale College was having its Commencement. Two days later three candidates, two from New Jersey and one from Maryland were admitted to the order of deacons and three others were advanced to the priesthood.

Professor Edward R. Hardy has brought to my attention a holograph document of Bishop Seabury's relating to the ordination of William Duke of Maryland on this occasion. The document contains the Bishop's signature and is reproduced in part elsewhere in this memoir. It reads as follows,

> Samuel by divine permission Bishop of the Episcopal Church in Connecticut; to our beloved in Christ, William Duke, Clerk, Greeting.
> We do by these presents Give and Grant unto You, in whose Fidelity, morals, sound Doctrine
> (Seal)   and Diligence we do fully confide, Our License and Authority, to continue only during our pleasure (or till a Bishop be regularly settled in the State where you shall officiate, to whose Ecclesiastical
> Samuel Bp. Authority you will of course be subject) to

perform the office of a Priest in the Church of
Ep.Chch.   Christ, more particularly in Queen Caroline's
Parish in Ann Arundel County in the State of
Connect.   Maryland in Reading the Common Prayer,
Preaching and performing all other Ecclesiastical Duties belonging to said office, according
to the Form prescribed in the Book of Common
Prayer and Administration of the Sacraments
in the Church of England, except where the said
Common Prayer is affected by the Civil Constitution of the United States. You having first
made and subscribed the declaration which we in
this Case required to be made and subscribed.

In Witness whereof we have caused our Episcopal Seal to be hereunto affixed at New Haven
in Connecticut the eighteenth day of October
1785, and in the first year of our Consecration. [2]

Commenting upon this Dr. Stokes writes, "This is a very
early document of American Episcopacy, since it was signed
within four months of Seabury's arrival in America. As he
was at the time the only Bishop of his Church in the colonies,
he had to perform some official acts outside of his specific
diocese. Maryland, to which this document has special reference, did not have an Episcopal Bishop of its own until
several years later. Seabury's habit of omitting his last
name in his official signature caused much comment and
amusement in Connecticut, as did also his use of the mitre
on important ecclesiastical occasions. The latter is symbol-
ically represented on the seal of the letter."[3]

The following year another meeting of note was held at
Derby at which certain important changes in the Liturgy were

adopted. As a result, a letter from Bishop Seabury was addressed to His Excellency Samuel Huntington, Esquire, Govenor of the State of Connecticut, telling him that the Prayer for the United States of America in Congress assembled, would be inserted in the Liturgy and used in celebration of Divine Service. In his reply the Governor acknowledged the changes in form and said, "I am happy to see the day when the spirit of bigotry seems almost extinguished, and religion is no longer prostituted as an engine in State policy to serve political parties and purposes."[4]

In his first year as Bishop, Seabury made numerous visits to neighborhoods outside of his jurisdiction, at Boston, Newport, Portsmouth and Hempstead. All were by invitation and no exception was taken except at his visit at Hempstead where as Bishop he ordained Mr. John Lowe of Virginia, both deacon and priest. Dr. Dix in his History of Trinity Church, New York, says that Bishop Seabury had no canonical right to officiate there and that the ordination caused no little annoyance in New York. There were, of course, no canons then existing in this country regulating his jurisdiction and there was no bishop having jurisdiction over the Church at Hempstead. It seems that Dr. Provoost of Trinity Church did object very strenuously to the procedure, imagining that the Bishop was trying to thwart the plan of having bishops consecrated in England. Seven years later Dr. Provoost, now Bishop.

ordained a clergyman for a congregation at Narragansett,
Rhode Island, a state which in 1790 had placed itself under
Bishop Seabury's jurisdiction. A minority of the congregation at Narragansett (now Wickford) had refused to concur,
and invited Bishop Provoost, then visiting there, to officiate.
Somewhat later a canon was enacted covering the situation.
William Seabury says that principle and duty ought to have
prevented Bishop Provoost from acceding to the request. At
a convention in Rhode Island Bishop Seabury did register a
complaint.

As noted, Drs. White and Provoost had been consecrated
in England in 1787. They landed in New York on April 7th of
that year. Soon after Bishop Seabury addressed letters to
both offering congratulations and asking for a meeting of the
three in order to promote unity between the States. In the
letter to Bishop Provoost he added an invitation to attend a
convocation of the Connecticut Clergy which was shortly to
be held in Stamford. Bishop White replied courteously, but
Bishop Provoost apparently did not reply at all. In fact, in
a letter to Dr. White a year before this, Dr. Provoost expressed a feeling towards Bishop Seabury which might account for his discourtesy. In this he says that it would be
highly improper to give any sanction to Bishop Seabury's
ordinations, that it would be an insult to the Church, et
cetera. Bishop Seabury, in a letter to Bishop Drummond of

Edinburgh, dated November 1, 1788, said of these two,
"Bishop White of Philadelphia, seems disposed to an Ecclesiastical Union, but will take no leading or active part to
bring it about. He will risk nothing; and Bishop Provoost
seems so elated with the honor of an English consecration
that he affects to doubt the validity of mine."[5]

W. J. Seabury says that Seabury was not quite correct
about White's attitude for the latter was the master mind in
the whole movement for union, working through the Rev. Dr.
Parker of Massachusetts, Seabury's good friend. Most of
the maneuvering came to a head in the General Convention of
August 1789 when it was, "Resolved; That a complete order
of Bishops, derived as well under the English as the Scots
line of Episcopacy, doth now subsist within the United States
of America, in persons of the Right Rev. William White, D.D.,
Bishop of the Protestant Episcopal Church in the State of
Pennsylvania, the Right Rev. Samuel Provoost, D.D., Bishop
of the said Church in the State of New York, and the Right
Rev. Samuel Seabury, D.D., of the said Church in the State
of Connecticut."[6]

At one stage of the proceedings, however, certain laymen
of the convention expressed scruples about Bishop Seabury as
a member, on the ground that he was receiving half-pay as a
retired British chaplain. Bishop White handled this question
adroitly by pointing out that it was compensation for past

services and not for any duties then expected of him and that
it did not prevent him from being a citizen with all rights.
The question was never again raised.

A matter of interest is concerned with prerogative. It
was important to Bishop Seabury for as we have seen the
validity of his consecration and all that it implied had been
subject to question in some quarters. To him, primacy in
the House of Bishops meant more to the Church of Connecticut than to him as a bishop. It is a matter of high interest
that the action which made Bishop Seabury the first to preside
in the House of Bishops originated with Bishop White. In 1792,
at a general convention held in Philadelphia, the matter of
seniority was changed making the presidency go by rotation.
In his journal, Seabury comments, "I had no inclination to
contend who should be the greatest in the kingdom of heaven,
and therefore readily consented to relinquish the Presidency
in the hands of Bp. Provoost. I thank God for his grace on
this occasion, and beseech him that no self exhaltation, or
envy of others may ever lead me into debate and contention,
but that I may ever be willing to be the least, when the peace
of his Church requires it. Amen."[7]

It is pleasant to record that at the convention in 1792,
the relations between Bishops Seabury and Provoost were
made friendly and that a considerable credit for this went to
Bishop White. He records that the two had never exchanged

visits and at his proposal Bishop Seabury without the least
hesitation agreed to visit Bishop Provoost and that he was
present when the meeting occurred. On the same day Provoost invited Seabury to dinner at which White and others
were present. Differences of opinion between these two
might persist afterwards but with friendship and understanding.

At the time of the consecration of Bishops White and
Provoost, the Connecticut Clergy became acutely aware that
if anything should deprive them of their beloved bishop they
would come under influences to the south which they had reason to suspect might be unfriendly to them. At a meeting in
Wallingford, February 27, 1787 they decided to send another
of their members to Scotland for consecration as Coadjutor
Bishop for the Diocese. The ever faithful Leaming was first
selected, but declined for reasons of health and the Rev.
Richard Mansfield of Derby was then appealed to. He likewise declined because of the burden of the journey. Then
Abraham Jarvis of Middletown was chosen to proceed. Bishop Seabury at once informed Bishop Skinner of this action
but by the time the prelates in Scotland had got around to
answering his letter the "English Consecrate", Bishops White
and Provoost, had arrived in America.

In reporting the sentiment of his Scottish brethren Bishop Skinner replied, (if) "these new Bishops either refuse to

hold communion with you, or grant it on terms with which
you cannot in conscience comply, there would be no room for
us to hesitate. But fain would we hope for better things of
these your American brethren, and there will be no occasion
for two separate communions among the Episcopalians of the
United States."[8]

Abraham Jarvis subsequently rose to the Episcopate but
it was not until a year and a half after Bishop Seabury's death.
On October 18, 1797, he was consecrated Bishop of Connecticut by Bishops, White, Provoost and Bass (of Massachusetts),
in Trinity Church, New Haven.

In the matter of dress on Church and other occasions,
Bishop Seabury seems to have attracted attention of the kind
he did with his baronial signature, mentioned early in our
story. The American Church had no provisions for the dress
of one of his office, but the Bishop had ideas of his own.
From his long sojourn in England, he was well informed as
to what had been there assigned to bishops as suitable to dis-
tinguish them from others, whether clergymen or laymen.
For him it was as natural to dress as a bishop in everyday
life as to wear the usual vestments of the Episcopal Clergy.
Apparently that is what he did on a visit to Boston in 1786,
for someone writing to a lady in New York referring to his
appearance said, "We have a Bishop in town named Seabury —
he dresses in a black shirt with a fore-flap hanging out, that's

one suit; at other times he appears in a black sattin gown;
white sattin sleeves, white belly band, with a scarlet knap-
sack at his back, and something resembling a pyramid on
his head."[9] W. J. Seabury suggests that only a man could
have written this letter for a woman would have known that
the sleeves were not "sattin". The pyramid was, of course,
the Bishop's Mitre. At that time the Church of England did
not call for a mitre as part of the usual Episcopal vestment
but previously it had been customary. Bishop Seabury may
or may not have seen a mitre in actual use in Scotland.
Beardsley says that the first time it was used by Bishop Seabury was at the consecration of the Church at New London,
September 20, 1787. William Seabury thinks that one was
probably of home manufacture.

The one which was used on later occasions was one which
the Rev. Charles Inglis obtained for him in London and is described by him in a letter appearing elsewhere in this book.
William Seabury's comment on the mitre of his distinguished
ancestor is, "It is curious to observe with what different
feelings men view such things as these. To Bishop Coxe, in
the fervor of the poetic imagination which produced the
Christian Ballads, the Mitre was a sacred relic. To Dean
Stanley in his visit to this Country some years ago it was the
survival of antequated absurdity. The Dean was extremely
amused with it. The moment I was presented to him he went

off into gentle ripples of hilarity at the remembrance of his
recent inspection of it. The amiable gentleman had probably
never before seen a Mitre except on the recumbent effigies
of his ancient Abbey, and he doubtless associated this one
with petrified Christianity. But Wisdom is justified with
all her children."[10]

When Seabury arrived in New London in 1785, there was
a congregation but no church, for that edifice had been destroyed by fire in the raid of the British forces in 1781 aided
by Benedict Arnold. The congregation remained without a
church until 1787, services being held in the meantime in
the Court House, and the Eucharist being celebrated every
Sunday in the parsonage which had been built in 1747. It was
there that, with his daughter Maria, the Bishop lived his remaining days. During his final years these two were joined
by his daughter Violetta, then widowed.

The busyness of Seabury's life as a bishop and rector of
a parish never seems to have abated until a day or two before
his death which occurred from a coronary seizure while
making a parochial call, February 25, 1796. Up until that
time, he seems to have had unusual good health. An interesting item in his journal of June 9, 1794 reads, "Rain prevented me from visiting Woodbridge according to appointment.
N.B. This is the first appointment in which I have failed
since I have been in Connecticut — such as been the goodness
of God."[11]

Some idea of Bishop Seabury's active life within his diocese is gained from his journal which tells of the visitations
and journeys from May 1791 to October 1795, a little over
four years. In that period he travelled 6666 miles and confirmed 1280 persons. Many of his journeys were made by
water in sailing vessels. Land journeys were made by stage-
coach, by sulky or by horseback. In his inventory his sulky
and harness were appraised at £ 12 and his horse at the same
figure. There were times when he could not afford a horse.
In a letter to Bishop White he excuses himself from making
a journey to Philadelphia on the ground that he was beyond
his present means. He had no horse at that time. Bishop
Seabury died intestate, his personal effects being estimated
at £ 275, presumably currency. He owned no property as
real estate. Whatever temporal prosperity he enjoyed during his lifetime came in the Westchester period before the
outbreak of war, but like many others who espoused the
cause of the Crown he lost almost all of whatever fortune he
possessed. After the war whatever was left was devoted to
his quest for the Episcopate.

During his sojourn in England his devoted friend James
Rivington advanced him funds to sustain himself and family.
Later on during his residence in New London various sums
were repaid and some monies used for this purpose came to
him from medical services rendered by him in New York

during the War. Following his consecration the fifty pounds
per year which he had been receiving as a missionary of the
Society, was withdrawn. From this time on a few devoted
friends in England joined in an annual contribution for his
support which was continued throughout his life.

The contribution of Samuel Seabury to the Episcopal
Church in America is inestimable. Seabury and White, as
Professor Hardy has pointed out, are the two great names
which have come down to us from its early years of existence
as the Protestant Episcopal Church in the United States of
America. Theirs was a fortunate combination of personali-
ties which is summed up for us in a quotation found in Norton's Life of Bishop Seabury. In reporting the General Convention of 1789 at which the constitution of the Church was
adopted we find the following, "Seabury was deliberate and
judicious; but withall resolute, efficient, unyielding. White
was gentle, conciliating, and prudent. What Seabury preached
with boldness, White recommended with suavity. White maintained, when Seabury was with him, what he would have con-
ceded by himself; and the opponents yielded to White, what
they would have contested with Seabury to the death. The
union of the Churches as one national Church could not have
been effected without White; but we owe it to Seabury that they
united on principles substantially sound. The Lord gave us
Peter to preach truth, as well as John to teach love."[12]

Moses Coit Tyler in his Literary History of the Revolution pays this tribute to Bishop Seabury; "He was a man
builded after an heroic pattern: a man of powerful frame, of
robust health, of tremendous energy—physical, mental,
moral; of great and varied experience in the affairs of life;
a physician, a theologian, a scholar, a terse and vigorous
writer; an orator of impassioned and commanding speech;
his mind firmly made up to clear and reverent conclusions
on all the great subjects that man, either alone or in society,
has to deal with. Moreover, there were in Seabury a singu-
lar courage of opinion, a downrightness of utterance, a necessity for the frank and emphatic expression of whatever convictions were within him, an inability to dodge important issues,
or to shuffle all responsibility, or to shirk a painful duty;
with all this, too, a grave and manly prudence, entire freedom from frothy zeal, or from light-headed impetuousity,
or from ambition for social martyrdom."[13]

Professor Tyler comes nearer the mark than any other
historian and his words should put to rest any superficial
judgments which give weight to such things as the Aspinwall
controversy, the Farmer letters, Seabury's toryism or the
wearing of the Mitre. We can be certain that if Bishop Seabury ever created an impression of unwarranted pride or
show it was but the result of his effort to place the Episcopate in what he considered its rightful position. As the first

American Bishop of his Church his responsibilities involved
the nurture of certain Church practices in a new and sometimes unfriendly environment, a responsibility which to him
was highly momentous. Misunderstanding and ridicule meant
little to him even when it came from certain elements in his
own State. Religious prejudice he had become aware of before he had outgrown boyhood in New London. To understand
it was part of his inheritance.

A most inspiring characteristic of Bishop Samuel Seabury was his ever cheerful disposition commented upon by
Myles Cooper, Chandler and others. He never allowed himself to be disheartened. His faith did not admit of discouragement. Writing as a refugee in New York under conditions
essentially that of siege he says, (I) "will not distrust the
goodness of God which has hitherto preserved me, nor render
myself unworthy of it by repining and discontent."[14]

William Jones Seabury's summary of the life of his distinguished forbear is one of devotion and praise and it is not
over-drawn; "A life of trouble and almost ceaseless strife;
of incessant labours and many sorrows; of much misunderstanding and most undeserved reproach! An Episcopate of
magnificent opportunities, of which he made the very most
that could be made under the restraining and hampering
limitations which surrounded him! And yet withal, a life of
ministry full of good tempered cheer, and self-surrendered

faithfulness; of absolute honesty, fearlessness and devotion; and singularly free from any trace of that self seeking and personal ambition, which sometimes taint the record of most glorious accomplishments! Such a life and ministry as well might make him ready to hear, whensoever it might come to him, the Angelic word of deliverance from the burden of the flesh— 'Go thou in thy way until the end be: for thou shalt rest, and stand in thy lot at the end of the day! Daniel XII, 13.' "[15]

Samuel Seabury, priest and physician, Bishop of Connecticut, is more than a great figure in the Episcopal Church of America. He remains of high importance in our history as a nation for out of his long, persistent, patient, skillful attentiveness to his earthly mission he is linked to all who profess Christianity on our shores.

Chapter Ten

FROM THE AUTHOR'S NOTEBOOK

Deacon John Seabury

Deacon John Seabury of Groton, Connecticut is given considerable mention in Frances M. Caulkins' History of New London. John and his brother Samuel came to Connecticut from Duxbury, Massachusetts, a little before 1700. Samuel purchased land in Lebanon and John settled at first in Stonington and in 1704 traded his farm there for one in Groton. Shortly after moving he was chosen deacon in the Congregational Church at Groton. Samuel, the father of the Bishop was the fifth of eight children and born July 6, 1706. Deacon John Seabury is probably buried at Pequonuck, in the town of Groton. His wife Elizabeth who died in 1771 at the age of 94, is buried at Stonington. According to Frances Caulkins the Bishop's father lived in the latter part of his rectorship at New London in a house on State Street which he built in 1737. It was sold by him in 1744 and in 1895 it was known as the Brainerd homestead.

Professor Edward R. Hardy says there is evidence that the name Seabury was pronounced in two syllables in the Bishop's time. In two letters written by Samuel Provoost, later Bishop of New York, one on October 25, 1785 and the other

December 8, in that same year, he refers to Bishop Seabury
as <u>Dr. Cebra</u>, which suggests this.

The Bishop's Family

During his pastorate at New London, the family of Bishop Seabury consisted of three daughters and three sons, all
adults. His wife had died during the war while he was a resident in New York. The oldest, Violetta Ricketts, born October 9, 1758, was married to Charles Nicol Taylor an officer
in the Royalist army. The second child was Abigail Mumford,
born February 12, 1760 who married Colin Campbell. The
third child named Mary, born July 20, 1761, was called
Maria by her father probably to avoid confusion with Mary
his wife. Samuel the next child was born October 29, 1765.
He became a doctor of medicine and married Frances Taber.
The next son was Edward, born October 5, 1767 who married
Lucretia Otis. The youngest was Charles, born May 29, 1770,
who married Ann Saltonstall of New London. The only de-
scendants of Bishop Seabury bearing his name trace through
Charles, the youngest son. Other descendants trace through
Violetta and Charles Taylor.

Samuel Johnson

Samuel Johnson is important in the Seabury story. For
a time he was the only Episcopal clergyman in Connecticut
and there seems to be little doubt that he was the spark that

ignited the "explosion" at Yale in 1722. As guide and coun-
selor to Thomas Chandler and Jeremiah Leaming he was
chiefly responsible for their turning to Episcopacy. Johnson
was born in Guilford, Connecticut, October 14, 1796 and
graduated from Yale in 1714, then the Collegiate School at
Saybrook. After the removal to New Haven he was the sole
tutor at the College for two years at which time he studied
theology. He was ordained as a Congregational minister to
the parish at West Haven, March 20, 1719.

As we have learned he went to England for Holy Orders
in 1722, returning to the Episcopal congregational at Stratford. Oxford gave him the degree of D.D. in 1743 and ten
years later he became the first president of King's College,
(now Columbia) New York. Following the death of his wife
in 1763 he retired to Stratford and took charge of his old
parish there. He died there January 6, 1772.

President Stiles says that the great Berkeley gifts came
to Yale through Samuel Johnson and Jared Eliot. The latter
was a trustee of the College. According to Stiles, "He
(Johnson) persuaded the Dean to believe that Yale College
would soon become Episcopal, and that they had received his
immaterial philosophy." (Stiles' Diary. January 22, 1772)[1]

Myles Cooper

Myles Cooper who was helpful to Bishop Seabury in so
many ways was born in England in 1735 and died at Edinburgh,

1785. He graduated at Oxford in 1760 and became a fellow
of Queens College. In 1762, at the instance of Thomas Sec-
ker, Archbishop of Canterbury, he came to America to assist President Johnson at King's College. He succeeded to
the presidency the next year.

Cooper was a pronounced loyalist and in 1774 published
a tract which aroused opposition especially among the students of the College. In 1775 a party of republicans set off
about midnight with the design of "seizing him in his bed,
shaving his head, cutting off his ears, slitting his nose,
stripping him naked, and setting him adrift."[2] The plot
being discovered, he escaped through a back window and the
next day went on board the English man-of-war, Kingfisher
in which he sailed to England. He was given two excellent
livings there, one in Edinburgh where he generally resided.
George Dudley Seymour in his essay on Leaming believes
that the plot was probably hatched in some tavern with a design to scare Cooper and that the conspirators relished the
success of their enterprise when they heard of his escape.

As we have seen, while Seabury was still fighting the
King's battles in Westchester, Doctors Cooper and Chandler
were safe in England. It was due to their efforts that Seabury received his chaplaincy and a gift of 50 pounds from a
fund they had helped to raise for needy clergymen in America. He was also indebted to them for his D.D. from Oxford
in 1777.

A tradition at Columbia is that Alexander Hamilton assisted Cooper's escape by delaying the rioters with a patri-
otic speech.   Cooper's living at Edinburgh was presumably
one of the English Chapels which existed there at that period
and not connected with the Scottish Episcopal Church.

Jeremiah Leaming

Jeremiah Leaming is the subject of a biographical sketch
written in 1928 by George Dudley Seymour at the time of the
presentation to the Glebe House of Leaming's Master of Arts
diploma conferred by King's College in 1785.   It was the gift
of Mr. and Mrs. James Hillhouse of New Haven.   Following
the Revolution Leaming became Rector of the Episcopal
Church in Stratford in 1784.   He served there until 1790
when he went to New York.   His final years were spent in the
home of Madame Hillhouse in New Haven.   She was the widow
of James A. Hillhouse and had been a friend of Leaming's
deceased wife.   Leaming died in New Haven in 1804.

In recording the famous Glebe House meeting on March
25, 1783 the historian E. E. Beardsley says that the two persons were selected, Jeremiah Leaming and Samuel Seabury.
However, W. J. Seabury writing later says that no supporting
evidence exists but that the convention might well have des-
ignated two candidates for the trust.   His assumption is that
the Connecticut Clergy regarded Seabury as the man for the
place but had so much respect for Leaming that they were

unwilling to overlook him and accordingly elected Seabury
with the understanding that Leaming should have the first offer. They were well aware that the ageing Leaming's infirmities might make him hesitate to embark on such a formid-
able undertaking.

James Wetmore

Shortly after graduating from Yale College in 1714, James
Wetmore became a minister to the Congregational Church at
Northfield, Massachusetts. In 1717 he removed to the Congregational Society at North Haven, Connecticut and was
there ordained September 30, 1718. As we have seen Wetmore united with his classmates Johnson and Browne in September 1722 in declaring for Episcopacy. He did not give up
his pastorate at once but on December 4th of that year the
group at North Haven voted to call a council, "To hear, consider and determine the difference between our pastor and
ourselves."[4]

As a result of those and other negotiations Wetmore re-
funded L 45 of the L 150 received as a life-settlement and resigned his pastorate. He then became catechist and school-
master for the Rev. William Vesey in New York and later
sailed for England and received ordination from Bishop Gibson. The Society appointed him as missionary to Rye, New
York in 1726 and there he remained until his death in 1760.
His charge included the villages of White Plains, Mamaroneck,

North Castle and Bedford and some missionary labors in
Connecticut.

Thomas Chandler

Thomas Bradbury Chandler after graduation from Yale
in 1745 spent the next year in New Haven presumably in further study. According to the Rev. Samuel Johnson it was during the latter part of this year that Chandler declared for Episcopacy. He taught school for a while in Woodstock, Massachusetts where his parents lived and where he was born. The
Society appointed him to be a catechist at Elizabeth, New
Jersey, in May, 1748. In 1751 he was ordained by Bishop
Sherlock of London. He then became rector at Elizabeth and
was highly successful in building up a large congregation.

On the approach of the Revolution he became a vigorous
pamphleteer and in the middle of 1775 he was forced to take
refuge on a British man-of-war in New York from whence he
sailed for England. His family was left in the rectory at Elizabeth where they remained for the entire war. After the proclamation of peace he was proposed for a bishopric at Nova
Scotia and remained for a time in England waiting for the
government to act in establishing that see. In 1786 when the
Episcopate was offered him his health was so far gone from a
cancerous affection that he could not accept the office. He
came back to Elizabeth and nominally, at least, retained his
old rectorship until his death in 1790.

Abraham Javis

Abraham Jarvis of Norwalk, Connecticut, graduated
from Yale College in 1761.[6] His family were members of
the Church of England and almost immediately after graduation he began to prepare himself for the ministry under the
Rev. Dr. Samuel Johnson. After ordination in England he became rector of Christ Church in Middletown. His active
ministry there was interrupted during the years of the Revolution but he was one of the earliest to resume church services and as we have seen was secretary of the famous meeting at Woodbury when Samuel Seabury was chosen for the
Episcopate. For a number of years Jarvis was chosen secretary of meetings of the Clergy, "as usual", which testifies to
his talent for this important office. On September 18, 1797,
a month before his consecration as Bishop of Connecticut
Yale conferred upon him the degree of Doctor of Divinity.
He is memorialized (by a tablet) in Trinity Church, New Haven, the scene of his consecration. His final resting place
is beneath the chancel in that Church.

Ezra Stiles

Ezra Stiles probably belongs but briefly in the Seabury
story but his importance as a commentator of his time has
endeared him to all historians. He was as eminent as a
patriot and Congregationalist as his college mate Seabury

was as a loyalist and Churchman and both were driven from
their parsonages by their respective enemies. It was while
he was exiled from his congregation at Newport, Rhode Island and living at Portsmouth, New Hampshire, that Stiles
accepted the presidency of Yale College. He became one of
her great presidents and doubtless was her most learned.
His famous diary began in 1769 carried on a daily record of
his life and times until his death in 1795. Stiles remarkable
Plan for a University complete with professional schools was
drafted while he was considering the acceptance of the Yale
presidency but it remained for his successor Timothy Dwight
to see it in reality. One of the new undergraduate colleges
recently constructed at Yale University bears the name of
Ezra Stiles.

On one occasion it is said that when Bishop Seabury was
attending a Commencement at Yale the suggestion was made
to President Stiles that the Bishop be invited to sit on the
stage, to which he replied, "We are all Bishops here, but if
there be room for another he can occupy it."[7]

Mason L. Weems

Mason Locke Weems and Edward Gantt, jr. were the
first candidates to receive Anglican ordination for service in
the United States after the change in the British law in 1784.
The former has become known facetiously as Parson Weems

and he did occupy rectorates in Maryland for six years. After 1792 for the next 31 years he was primarily a book seller wandering up and down the Eastern seaboard. He was also an editor, compiler, writer and "stepfather" to a number of books. His Life and Memorable Actions of George Washington (c. 1800) went through 70 editions including five in German. In the fifth edition (1806), the "hatchet and cherry tree story" appeared first in book form giving that work an immortality he would not have relished. An interesting account of his various activities is found in volume XIX of the Dictionary of American Biography.

The Glebe House

The Glebe House at Woodbury, Connecticut,[8] at the time of the famous meeting of the Connecticut Clergy was the home of the Rev. John Rutgers Marshall who took up residence there in 1771 and remained until some time after the Revolution. He was trained for college by the Rev. Dr. Samuel Johnson and after graduation from King's College, New York, went to London for ordination. As Rector of St. Paul's, Woodbury, he remained at his post all through the war suffering much persecution although there is no evidence that he was a pronounced tory. After the war he seems to have gotten along well with his Puritan neighbors.

The Glebe House was erected early in the town's settlement, around 1660. It consisted at first of two rooms and

a large field-stone chimney.   The house was enlarged about
the time of the founding of St. Paul's Parish in 1750.   The
Reverend Marshall used the house as a glebe, that is, as
part of his benefice.   He was part owner of the house until
1786 at which time it was sold to augment a fund to erect a
church.   Marshall and his family then lived in a parsonage.
In 1892 the Glebe House was presented as a Christmas gift to
Bishop John Williams of Connecticut.   Today it is recognised
as a shrine of early Episcopacy in America and is maintained
by the Seabury Society for the Preservation of the Glebe House,
a society which was formed in 1925 by then Suffragan Bishop
Acheson.

St. James's Church, New London

The first Episcopal Church in New London, Connecticut,
was opened in 1732 and was called the Episcopal Church of
New London.   It became known as St. James's Church in 1741.
The first resident rector was the Rev. Samuel Seabury, the
father of Bishop Seabury.   During the Revolution the Rev.
Matthew Graves was rector and because of his insistence to
read prayers for the King and royal family he was obliged to
seek refuge behind the British lines and there became a chaplain.   After this the church was closed for three years.   In
1781 the church was destroyed at the burning of New London
by the British.   A second church on the corner of Church
and Main Streets was built following the coming of Bishop

Seabury as Rector of the Church.

The present St. James's Church was consecrated, June 11, 1850, and was one of the first churches in America to use the Gothic type of architecture. The architect, Richard Upjohn was one of the foremost of his day. It is a large church and an impressive one. There are here four memorials to Bishop Samuel Seabury, a chapel bearing his name, a memorial near the chancel, a plaque in Hallam Chapel marking his tomb, and a monument on the grounds.

The Duché Portrait

The Duché portrait of Bishop Seabury has an interesting background other than that which has been told. The Rev. Dr. Duché at the beginning of the Revolution was Rector of Christ Church, Philadelphia, and at first was apparently sympathetic to the patriots as he was officiating chaplain at the first session of the Congress. Later he transferred his residence to London and was succeeded in both positions by the Rev. William White, afterward Bishop of Pennsylvania. When White assumed the latter office Duché returned to Philadelphia. The portrait probably came with him for it was presented by Bishop White to the Diocese of Connecticut on behalf of the artist's sister. It is now at Trinity College, Hartford. In addition to the copy made by Mildred Jordon which is now at Yale, another by Mr. Yewell is at the General Theological Seminary in New York. William J. Seabury says that two

other portraits were painted in this country after the Bishop's
return, one by Ralph Earle and the other by an unknown artist.
At the time of the writing of his memoir (1908) the Earle
portrait was in the possession of Mr. Samuel Seabury Bell
and the other in his own possession.

The Bishop's Mitre

The making of the Mitre seems to have been quite an undertaking. Writing from London, September 14, 1786, the
Rev. Dr. Charles Inglis tells of the efforts which he had been
made to comply with Bishop Seabury's wish to have a Mitre
as part of his vestments. He writes,–

"Agreeably to your desire, I called upon Mr. Stone about
the Mitre. As no Mitres are worn by our Bishops in England,
the manufacture of them is consequently little known. Neither
Stone, nor any other person I could hear of, had ever made
one. However, I told Stone he must try his hand. He and I
have consulted together at least a dozen times; and we also
called in a very ingenious embroiderer to assist us. After
consulting a variety of books, cuts, monuments, &c (for no
real Mitre was to be found) we at last fixed on the size, materials and manner of execution; all of which I hope will meet
your approbation. The size I fancy is large enough. The
materials are paste-board covered with black sattin; a cross
in gold embroidery, with a Glory around it in front; and a
crown of thorns, in gold embroidery, on the back part. The

two lobes, if I may so call them, lined with white silk; and
each pointed with a gilt cross, such as is usual in the Mitres
of Bishops. The lower part is bound with a handsome black
lace, and inside lined with black thin silk. The ribbons with
which it ties down, are purple and each pointed with a bit of
gold lace. My wish was to have it decent and respectable;
without anything tawdry, or very expensive about it. What
the expense will be I know not, and shall order the bill to be
put up with the Mitre, by which you will learn it – it cannot be
very great; and therefore if this Mitre does not please or fit
you, the next may be made more to your mind."[10]

I am indebted to Professor Edward R. Hardy for the following notes on Mitres."[11] The general story is this – pro-
perly a Bishop wears a mitre with eucharistic vestments or
a cope, not with the more informal robes, rochet and chimere,
used by our Bishops on most accasions. Some 17th-century
monuments show Anglican Bishops in chimere and mitre
(only one in cope and mitre I believe), which may indicate
that it was so worn. The latest reference to the use of a mitre in the Church of England before the modern revival is at
the funeral of George II in 1760 when the Dean of Westmin-
ster, who was also a Bishop is mentioned as carrying his.
A proper mitre is collapsible – as Dr. Rockwell who used to
teach History at Union Seminary once pointed out to me. A
Bishop as a travelling official has a folding hat, a folding

chair, and a stick. Being based on pictures etc., such as the
coats-of-arms on Episcopal carriages, Seabury's mitre as
Canon West of New York pointed out to me is what is called
a coachman's mitre, that is, solid. Bishop Claggett of Maryland, the one Bishop whom Seabury helped to consecrate,
used a similar mitre; but I doubt whether any other Anglican
Bishop took up the custom until about 1870. J. Wickham
Legg, (English Church Life from the Restoration to the
Tractarian Movement, 1914, p.371) notes that the Bishops
carried mitres at the coronation of George II, 1727. Hieuru-
gia Angelica 3 vols., 1902-4, a collection of details of services has in vol. III a picture of the mitre of Bishop
Wren of Ely, (preserved at Pembroke College, Cambridge),
who died in 1667—very much like Seabury's, and notes, vol.
I, that in the Restoration period mitres were regularly carried with other insignia at Episcopal funerals, and often
represented in effigies on tombs—sometimes in the older
costume of cope and mitre, more often with the usual Angel-
ican chimere such as Seabury wore; Archbishop Sharp of
York, who died in 1713, seems to be one of the latest cases—
there is a statement that the Archbishop of Cashel in Ireland
wore the mitre at a funeral in 1781; but still one can understand why Inglis said he could find no real mitre, pp. 227-
35 from Coxe's Christian Ballads, 1858, p.210. Hierurgia
quotes a description of Seabury at his first ordination "wear-
his scarlet hood and that mitre", p.234.

Memorials to Bishop Seabury

In addition to the memorials already mentioned relating
to Bishop Seabury the Altar from his church in New London
and the Chalice and Paten which he used there is now preserved at the Berkeley Divinty School in New Haven. Over
the door of the Church Missions House in New York is a
stone relief figure of the Bishop. At St. Andrew's Church
in Aberdeen, Scotland is a wing of a building which bears his
name and at the University of Aberdeen a tablet adorns a wall
bearing a Mitre and inscribed to him. W. J. Seabury speaks
of other memorials in stained glass but does not specify. At
St. Paul's Church in Rome he is commemorated in a lancet
window. At the hundredth anniversary of Bishop Seabury's
death at a service at the St. James's Church, New London,
the Rev. W. J. Seabury who participated records the wearing
of the Bishop's surplice.

Cleric Physicians

The practice of medicine by Samuel Seabury along with
his parish activities was not unusual before and during his
time in the Colonies. He had, in fact, a better training in
medicine than many doctors of his time for study abroad was
a rarity with young men in apprenticeship in medicine. Medicine combined with theology dates back to the time of our
earliest New England ministers. The last of New England's
great cleric physicians was Jared Eliot of Killingworth,

(Clinton) Connecticut. His father the Rev. Joseph Eliot and
his grandfather the Rev. John Eliot, called the Apostle to the
Indians, both practised medicine. Jared Eliot in addition to
being a great figure in the Congregational Church was the
outstanding medical teacher of his day in Connecticut.

There is evidence that after his consecration Seabury
practised to some extent in New London. At the time of his
death one notice in the public press said, "the poor will miss
him as a physician and friend."[10]

The Scottish Church and Connecticut

The Episcopal Church of Scotland and the Church in
Connecticut have preserved the strong ties of friendship
which began so long ago. Within recent years these have
been greatly strengthened through interchanges seen in the
following, —In 1884, Bishop John Williams, Bishop of Connecticut attended at Aberdeen the centennial observance of
Bishop Seabury's consecration, and on that occasion presented the gifts of a Chalice and Paten to the Cathedral. In
return the Bishop of Connecticut was presented with a handsome Pastoral Staff now deposited at the Cathedral in Hartford and used by the Bishops of Connecticut in services there.

On June 28, 1948, Bishop Frederick G. Budlong, Bishop
of Connecticut and Bishop Walter H.Gray, Bishop Coadjutor
of Connecticut went to Aberdeen and presented Flagons for
the wine and water for the Service of Holy Communion,

supplementing the gifts of Bishop Williams. It is of interest that St. Andrew's Cathedral, Aberdeen, gives the Bishop of Connecticut the privilege of nominating two Honorary Canons of the Cathedral and acts upon nomination from him for an Honorary Canonry in the Cathedral at Hartford.

On July 25, 1953, Bishop Walter H. Gray, Bishop of Connecticut participated at Aberdeen at the installation of the Rev. Dr. John V. Butler, Jr., as an American Canon in Aberdeen. He is now the Dean of the Cathedral of St. John the Divine in New York. On April 25, 1956, Bishop Gray at the request of the Primus of the Episcopal Church of Scotland served as the Presenting Bishop for the Rt. Rev. Edward F. Easson as Bishop of Aberdeen and Orkney. As far as is known it was the first instance of an American Bishop participating in a Scottish consecration.

On August 3, 1958, Bishop Gray, Bishop of Connecticut, at the request of the Bishop of Aberdeen and Orkney preached at St. Andrew's Cathedral, Aberdeen and in St. John's Church, Longside.

NOTES

Chapter I

[1]E. E. Beardsley, History of the Episcopal Church in Connecticut, 2d ed. (New York, 1869) p. 19

[2]Ibid, p. 21, 22

[3]F. B. Dexter, Biographical Sketches of the Graduates of Yale College with the Annals of the College History (New York, 1885) p. 203

[4]Beardsley, p. 33

[5]Ibid, p. 34

[6]Ebenezer Baldwin, Annals of Yale College from its Foundation, to the Year 1831, 2d ed. (New Haven, 1838) p. 37 38

[7]Beardsley, p. 29

[8]H. L. Sibley, Biographical Sketches of Those who attended Harvard College, v. 1, 1722-25 (Boston, 1945) p. 440

Chapter II

[1]F. B. Dexter, Biographical Sketches of the Graduates of Yale College with Annals of the College History (New York, 1896) p. 6

[2]Ibid, p. 7

[3]Ibid, p. 18

[4]A. P. Stokes, Memorials of Eminent Yale Men (New Haven, 1914) p. 45

[5]Ebenezer Baldwin, Annals of Yale College from its Foundation to the Year 1831, 2d ed. (New Haven, 1838) p. 90

[6]E. E. Beardsley, Life and Correspondence of Samuel Seabury (Boston, 1881) p. 5

[7]W. J. Seabury, Memoir of Samuel Seabury (New York, 1908) p. 9

[8]Ibid, p. 8

[9]Dexter, vol. 1, p. 241

[10]Seabury, p. 29, 30

Chapter Three

[1]W. J. Seabury, Memoir of Bishop Seabury (New York, 1908) p. 54, 55

[2]Ibid, p. 55, 56

[3]Ibid, p. 56

[4]Ibid, p. 56, 57

[5]Ibid, p. 57, 58

[6]Ibid, p. 62

[7]Ibid, p. 63, 64

[8]Ibid, p. 67

[9]Ibid, p. 70

[10]E. E. Beardsley, Life and Correspondence of the Rt. Rev. Samuel Seabury, D. D. (Boston, 1881) p. 12

Chapter Four

[1]E. E. Beardsley, Life and Correspondence of the Rt. Rev. Samuel Seabury, D. D. (Boston, 1881) p. 22

[2]G. O. Trevelyan, The American Revolution (New York, 1903) v. 1, pt. 2, p. 339

[3]Ibid, p. 338

[4]C. H. Vance, Introduction to Letters of a Westchester

Farmer (White Plains, N. Y., 1930) p. 12-13

[5]Ibid, p. 17

[6]W. J. Seabury, Memoir of Bishop Seabury (New York, 1908) p. 113, 114

[7]Ibid, p. 79

[8]Ibid, p. 84

[9]Ibid, p. 86-88

[10]Vance, p. 17

[11]Beardsley, p. 26

[12]Trevelyan, p. 339

[13]Ibid, p. 339

[14]Beardsley, p. 27

[15]Ibid, p. 30

[16]Barrett Wendell, A Literary History of America (New York, 1901) p. 110

[17]Ibid, p. 111

[18]Vance, p. 24

[19]Beardsley, p. 32

[20]Ibid, p. 33, 34

[21]Ibid, p. 35

[22]Ibid, p. 39

[23]Ibid, p. 42

[24]Ibid, p. 44

[25]Seabury, p. 169

Chapter Five

[1]John Fiske, The American Revolution (Boston, 1902) v. 2, p. 355

[2]E. E. Beardsley, Life and Correspondence of Samuel Seabury (Boston, 1881) p. 49

[3]Ibid, p. 51

[4]Ibid, p. 52, 53

[5]Ibid, p. 54

[6]Ibid, p. 60

[7]Ibid, p. 66, 67

[8]Ibid, p. 67, 68

[9]J. N. Norton, The Life of the Rt. Rev. Samuel Seabury, D. D. (New York, 1859) p. 41

Chapter Six

[1]Jared Eliot, The Blessings Bestowed on them that Fear God. (Sermon) New London, 1739

[2]F. M. Caulkins, History of New London, Connecticut, New London, 1895, p. 355

[3]Henry Bronson, Medical History and Biography, New Haven, n. d. p. 13, (from the papers of the New Haven Colony Historical Society, vol. II)

Chapter Seven

[1]E. E. Beardsley, Life and Correspondence of Samuel Seabury (Boston, 1881) p. 71

[2]Ibid, p. 103

[3]Ibid, p. 105

[4]Ibid, p. 106-7

[5]Ibid, p. 108-9

[6]Ibid, p. 110

[7]Ibid, p. 115-116

[8]W. J. Seabury, Memoir of Bishop Seabury (New York, 1908) p. 208-210

[9]Ibid, p. 226, 229

[10]Beardsley, p. 130-131

[11]Seabury, p. 225

[12]Ibid, p. 226

[13]Beardsley, p. 127

[14]Seabury, p. 226

[15]Beardsley, p. 129

[16]Ibid, p. 131

[17]Ibid, p. 133

[18]Ibid, p. 138

[19]Seabury, p. 229

[20]Ibid, p. 231-232

[21]Beardsley, p. 142

[22]Ibid, p. 142

Chapter Eight

[1]E. E. Beardsley, Life and Correspondence of the Rt. Rev. Samuel Seabury, D.D. (Boston, 1881) p. 153

[2]Ibid, p. 145-146

[3]Ibid, p. 157

[4]Ibid, p. 150-153

[5]Herbert Thoms, The Doctors of Yale College, 1702-1815 (Hamden, Conn., 1958) p. 10

[6]W. J. Seabury, Memoir of Bishop Seabury (New York, 1908) p. 392

[7]Beardsley, p. 182

[8]Ibid, p. 183-185

[9]Ibid, p. 169

[10]Seabury, p. 265-269

Chapter Nine

[1]E. E. Beardsley, Life and Correspondence of Samuel Seabury, D.D. (Boston, 1881) p. 219

[2]MSS now in the Yale Memorabilia Collection, Yale University Library

[3]A. P. Stokes, Memorials of Eminent Yale Men (New Haven, 1914) v. 1, p. 50

[4]W. J. Seabury, Memoir of Bishop Seabury (New York, 1908) p. 287

[5]Ibid, p. 309

[6]Ibid, p. 313-314

[7]Ibid, p. 361

[8]E. E. Beardsley, History of the Episcopal Church in Connecticut (New York, 1869) p. 400

[9]W. J. Seabury, p. 361

[10]Ibid, p. 365

[11]Ibid, p. 407

[12]J. N. Norton, The Life of the Rt. Rev. Samuel Seabury, D.D. (New York, 1859) p. 85

[13]A. P. Stokes, p. 48

[14]E. E. Beardsley, Life and Correspondence of Samuel Seabury, D.D. (Boston, 1881) p. 53

[15]W. J. Seabury, p. 409-410

Chapter Ten

[1]F. B. Dexter, The Literary History of Ezra Stiles, D.D., LL. D. (New York, 1901) p. 206

[2]G. D. Seymour, The Reverend Josiah Leaming (Woodbury, 1928) p. 29

[3]F. B. Dexter, Biographical Sketches of the Graduates of Yale College (New York, 1885) p. 134

[4]Ibid, vol. 2 (New York, 1896) p. 23

[5]Ibid, p. 701

[6]Ibid, p. 92-97

[7]W. J. Seabury, Memoir of Bishop Seabury (New York, 1908) p. 362

[8]The Birthplace of American Episcopacy, A History of St. Paul's Church and the Glebe House (Pamphlet, Woodbury, n. d.)

[9]St. James's Church – Seat of the First Episcopal Bishopric in America. (Pamphlet, New London, n. d.)

[10]W. J. Seabury, p. 353

[11]Personal Communication

[12]W. J. Seabury, p. 353

GENERAL BIBLIOGRAPHY

Baldwin, Ebenezer. Annals of Yale College from its Foundation to the Year 1831 (New Haven, 1838)

Beardsley, E. E. History of the Episcopal Church in Connecticut (New York, 1869)

Beardsley, E. E. Life and Correspondence of the Right Reverend Samuel Seabury, D. D. (Boston, 1881)

Caulkins, F. M. History of New London, Connecticut (New London, 1895)

Chambers, Walter. Samuel Seabury, A Challenge (New

Dexter, F. B. Biographical Sketches of the Graduates of Yale College. vol. 1-2 (New York, 1885)

Dictionary of American Biography (New York, 1936) Edited by Dumas Malone

Fiske, John. The American Revolution (Boston, 1891)

Green, J. R. A Short History of the English People (New York, n. d.)

Hallam, R. A. Annals of St. James's, New London (Hartford, 1873)

Johnston, H. P. Yale and Her Honor-roll in the American Revolution (New York, 1888)

Norton, J. N. Life of the Rt. Rev. Samuel Seabury, D. D. (New York, 1859)

Rand, Benjamin. Berkeley's American Sojourn (Cambridge, Mass., 1932)

Seabury, W. J. Memoir of Bishop Seabury (New York, 1908)

Seymour, G. D. The Reverend Jeremiah Leaming of Connecticut (Woodbury, 1928)

Stokes, A. P. Memorials of Eminent Yale Men (New Haven, 1914)

Thoms, Herbert. The Doctors Jared of Connecticut (Hamden, Conn., 1958)

---- ----. The Doctors of Yale College 1702-1815 and the Founding of the Medical Institution (Hamden, Conn., 1960)

Trevelyan, G. O. The American Revolution (New York, 1903)

Vance, C. H. Letters of a Westchester Farmer (1774-1775) (White Plains, 1930)

Woolsey, T. D. An Historical Discourse Pronounced before the Graduates of Yale College, August 14, 1850 (New Haven, 1850)

INDEX